Raising Rabbits Indoors

The Complete House Rabbit Care Guide

Includes facts on breeding, indoor rabbit habitat, training, behavior, diet, health, diseases, showing, and breeders by breed

By Anita Haley

Raising Rabbits Indoors

The Complete House Rabbit Care Guide

Includes facts on breeding, indoor rabbit habitat, training, behavior, diet, health, diseases, showing, and breeders by breed

Author: Anita Haley

ISBN 978-1-927870-44-0

Copyright © 2013 Ubiquitous Publishing

ubiquitouspublishing.com
Published in Canada

Printed in the USA

Foreword

Rabbits are one of the many species of companion animals that have suffered from the "outside" animal prejudice of days gone by. If effective ways can be found to manage the elimination needs of any species, they can live indoors, as evidenced by the many pet owners who keep everything from chickens to pigs as house pets.

With rabbits, this "problem" is no problem at all. Bunnies are creatures of habit. They pick a spot where they like to "go" and they "go" back there over and over again. Once you have identified that spot (typically a corner), you simply put a litter box in place and you're done. While this process may take a while with younger rabbits, older bunnies basically thank you for the nice "renovation" and go right on handling their business as before.

A bigger issue with house rabbits is that the creatures are, by nature, chewers and diggers. If a rabbit finds a loose bit of carpet in a corner, game over. In just a few minutes that corner will be an entrance to a tunnel, and you'll be extricating your bunny from his freshly discovered digs.

Almost anything is fair game for the chewing. Don't even think about leaving that stack of paperback books on the floor. For that matter, fear for the legs of the coffee table. If you're going to have a house rabbit, you will need to rabbit proof. Many owners opt to design a rabbit-proof room.

Foreword

House rabbits do not just sit in their cages all day. They need at least 2 hours of exercise -- and be prepared. A rabbit having fun can be a rowdy critter. The image of bunnies placidly sitting and chewing on hay is only part of the picture. Wait until you see your rabbit toss a toy in the air the first time, or go rocketing around the room in the rabbit version of what cat owners call "zooming."

While not all rabbits like to be held, they are still wonderfully intelligent and affectionate animals -- and sometimes, they're just plain funny. It's also highly likely that if you have a larger rabbit and he's just plain had enough of the family dog, Fido will get a dose of bunny bullying. Those big hind legs on a rabbit are quite good for kicking, and rabbits know how to use them when they need to.

The most important thing you can do before buying a bunny is to fully understand what is involved in keeping one as a house pet. To fail to do so is a disservice to you, your family, and most importantly, the rabbit.

The text of this book provides a comprehensive overview of selecting and caring for a house rabbit. Bear in mind, however, that this is a broad topic and that rabbit lovers are an enthusiastic genre of pet owner. This guide will get you started with a solid foundation of information on house rabbits, but even if you've kept bunnies for 20 years, there's always more to learn, -- which for many rabbit enthusiasts is just one of the reasons they love their long-eared companions so much.

Acknowledgments

I've been around pet rabbits all my life. From the time I was nine years old, I had my first bunnies - Spotty and Snowball, that my parents intended to keep out in the cold winters in a custom-built hutch. On weekends, we would bring them in the basement to play, and eventually, to live.

I want to thank all the people I've met along the journey - from introductions to the first breeders who convinced me to take the bunnies I fell in love with home, my parents who allowed it, the vets and people in my community who passed on great advice along the way, the bloggers who gave knowledgeable advice when I needed it, as well as my immediate family who are also bunny-lovers.

Without all these people, this book would not have been written.

Table of Contents

Table of Contents

Table of Contents

Table of Contents

Table of Contents

Chapter 1 – An Introduction to Rabbits

People new to the idea of keeping a companion rabbit are often taken aback by the sheer variety these animals offer in

terms of size, quality of coat, and type of personality.

There is literally a rabbit out there for just about anyone willing to learn how to care for them, physically and emotionally, which is the point of this book.

Difference Between Rabbits and Hares

Although both rabbits and hares are in the order

Chapter 1 – An Introduction to Rabbits

Lagomorpha and the family *Leporidae*, hares belong to the genus *Lepus*. They differ from rabbits in several key ways.

Hares:

- are larger,
- faster,
- have big back feet,
- sport stronger, longer hind legs,
- and have black markings on their fur.

Hares are not domesticated, and unlike all species of rabbits (except cottontails), they live on the ground in simple nests. Young hares are called "leverets".

There are eight genera of rabbits, all of which can be domesticated:

Pentalagus - Amami Rabbit
Bunolagus - Riverine Rabbit
Nesolagus - This genus includes three species of striped rabbits.
Romerolagus - Volcano Rabbit
Brachylagus - Pygmy Rabbit
Sylvilagus - Cottontail
Oryctolagus - European Rabbit
Poelagus - Bunyoro

Rabbits come in a broad range of physical sizes from pygmy to giant. Their fur can be slick or long haired, and their personality timid to aggressive. Young rabbits are called "kits".

Select Rabbit Breeds

The following are some of the more popular of the 50 or so breeds of rabbits typically shown and sold in the United States and Europe.

In general, the smaller breeds are most popular as pets, but all types of rabbits have their passionate advocates. Always fully research any breed in which you are interested before you bring the rabbit into your home!

Small: Four to Eight Pounds

American Fuzzy Lop - These small rabbits with their flat faces and lopped ears are bred in a variety of colors. They weigh 3-4 pounds (1.3 – 1.8 kg). As a "wool" breed, they require daily grooming.

Britannia Petite - Tiny and compact, with trim bodies and narrow heads, these rabbits weigh 2-2.5 pounds (0.9 – 1.1 kg). They have some tendency to be hyper and may bite if they are not handled carefully. Be cautious about allowing younger children to have this breed as a pet due to the Britannia Petite's fine bone structure.

Dutch - At a weight of 3-5 pounds (1.36 – 2.26 kg), Dutch rabbits are compact and well rounded. They are one of the oldest of all rabbit breeds and are an especially good choice as pets because they do quite well with children. They come in six color varieties.

Dwarf Hotot - These striking white rabbits with their distinctive black eye rings weigh 2-3 pounds (0.9 – 1.36 kg) and are pleasantly round and compact.

English Angora - A fluffy, funny looking fuzz ball, the English Angora takes a great deal of daily grooming, but for people prepared to do a lot of brushing, the Angora is a very companionable and sweet breed. They weigh 5-7 pounds (2.26 – 3.17 kg).

Florida White - The stereotypical white rabbit, the Florida White has a round head, round body, and short erect ears. Their eyes are pink or ruby. They weigh 4-6 pounds (1.8 – 2.7 kg).

Havana- These rabbits come in blue, black, and chocolate. Their bodies are wide at the shoulder, but short overall. They are especially prized for their plush coats and make nice pets due to their compact weight of 4.5 to 6.5 pounds (2.04 – 2.9 kg).

Himalayan - The Himalayan is a white rabbit with colored ears, nose, feet, and tail in black, blue, lilac, or chocolate. Their bodies are long, with narrow heads highlighted by short, erect ears. They weigh 2.5 to 4.5 pounds (1.1 – 2.04 kg).

Holland Lop - A highly popular breed, the Holland Lop's head is slightly flat with a prominent crown, or ridge of cartilage between the ears. They have soft, beautifully fur and charming droopy ears. They weigh 2.75 to 4 pounds (1.25 – 1.8 kg).

Jersey Wooly - Round and compact with dense fur, Jersey Wooly rabbits require a fair amount of grooming. They are bred in many colors, and loved for their compact, round, cuddly bodies in a weight range of 2.75 to 3.5 pounds (1.25 – 1.58 kg).

Lionhead - Originally a Belgian breed, developed in England, these fuzzy, funny little rabbits have medium length fur that is 2-3 inches (5.08 – 7.62 cm) in length. They do require a good bit of grooming, but at 3-3.75 pounds (1.36 – 1.7 kg) and with an adorable appearance, they are highly popular.

Mini Plush Lop - Considered an exceptional choice as a pet at a size of just 2.5 to 3.5 pounds (1.1 – 1.58 kg) , the Mini Plush Lop was created in the 1990s. They are affectionate and loyal, with soft, dense fur.

Mini Rex - An attractive breed with velvet-like fur in many colorations, the Mini Rex is compact with narrow shoulders and upright ears. They weigh from 2.75 to 4.5 pounds (1.25 – 2.04 kg).

Netherland Dwarf - With their glossy fur and multiple colorations, Netherland Dwarf rabbits are good pets, but perhaps not for children since they do have a tendency to nip if mishandled. They weigh 1.75 to 2.5 pounds (0.79 – 1.1 kg).

Polish - Compact rabbits with short, upright ears, Polish rabbits have short, dense fur in blue, chocolate, white, or broken patterns. They weigh 2 to 3.5 pounds (0.9 – 1.58 kg).

Standard Chinchilla - One of the larger of the "small" breeds at 5-7 pounds (2.26 – 3.17 kg), the Standard Chinchilla is a chubby little bunny with long, upright ears. The individual hairs of their coats are blue at the base, graduating to pearl, and tipped in black.

Medium: Eight to Ten Pounds

American Sable - With a long, medium-sized body, the American Sable's nose, ears, feet, and tail are all dark brown. The ears are erect and long. Body weight is 7-10 pounds (3.17 – 4.53 kg).

Belgian Hare - Although the Belgian Hare looks like its long-legged relative, it is a rabbit, but with a lean body and big, upright ears. They weigh 6 to 9.5 pounds (2.72 – 4.3 kg).

English Spot - A whimsically spotted little bunny with a butterfly mark on its nose and distinctive eye rings, the English Spot is white with colored marks like a Dalmatian (although they come in seven color varieties including black.) The English Spot can be prone to a somewhat nervous temperament. These rabbits weigh 6-8 pounds (2.72 – 3.62 kg).

Harlequin - French in origin, Harlequins have bi-colored, banded bodies and heads. They are rounded in conformation, with upright, long ears and a body weight of 7 to 9.5 pounds (3.17 – 4.3 kg).

Lilac - A lovely purplish gray in color, the Lilac is a roundish rabbit with a narrow head and erect, medium-length ears. They weigh 5.75 to 8 pounds (2.6 – 3.62 kg).

Palomino -These golden rabbits also come in lynx coloration. Their bodies are medium in length as are their upright ears. They weigh 8-10.5 pounds (3.62 – 4.76 kg).

Rex - A lovely, rounded rabbit with large erect ears, the Rex has a plush coat with the feel of finest velvet. They weigh 7.5 to 10.5 pounds (3.4 – 4.76 kg).

Large: Ten to Twelve Pounds

American Chinchilla - Each hair on the American Chinchilla is slate blue with pearl banding in the center and black tips. Medium and well-rounded rabbits with long, upright ears, they weigh 9 to 12 pounds (4.08 – 5.4 kg).

Champagne d' Argent - These rabbits have a coat that slowly changes as they age from black to silver. Their ears are long and erect, capping a slightly elongated head set on a medium length body. They weigh 9 to 12 pounds (4.08 – 5.4 kg).

English Lop - Beloved for their floppy ears that are often as much as 12 inches (30.48 cm) in length, the English Lop is a companionable breed, but for more experienced rabbit owners.

They are somewhat more susceptible than other breeds to both injury and disease if not cared for properly. They weigh 9 to 12 pounds (4.08 – 5.4 kg).

French Lop - The French is the biggest of all the lop breeds, with a well-muscled body, wide head, and thick ears. They are bred in many colors and are well loved for their calm, affectionate disposition. French Lops weigh 10-14 pounds (4.53 – 6.35 kg).

New Zealand - A suburb pet, the New Zealand comes in black, red, and white. Their ears are upright and medium in length. They weigh 9 to 12 pounds (4.08 – 5.4 kg).

Giant Rabbits: Twelve Pounds and Above

Flemish Giant - Absolutely massive and wonderful rabbits in colorations including black, blue, fawn, light grey, sandy, steel, or white, the Flemish Giant takes some strength to handle, but is very popular as a pet for the right owner. They weigh 14 pounds (6.35 kg) and above.

Giant Chinchilla - A somewhat smaller "giant" at 12 pounds (5.4 kg) and above, the Giant Chinchilla has fur banded in slate, pearl, and black. Their full bodies are long and they have lovely, erect ears.

Chapter 2 – Buying a Rabbit

Bringing any pet into your life and home is a serious responsibility. Especially with a sensitive animal like a rabbit, it's imperative that you understand what you're getting yourself into — especially since you're interested in having a *house* rabbit.

What to Know Before You Buy

Long before you ever contact a breeder and explore buying your bunny, you must honestly answer all the following questions.

Do I have the time for a rabbit?

House rabbits need at least 2-3 hours of exercise per day. While multiple rabbits will play happily with one another, a single pet will rely solely on you for affection and interaction.

You will also need to set aside at least an hour a day for doing your bunny's housekeeping. This includes changing the litter in the rabbit's box, cleaning the cage, feeding and watering, and performing any necessary grooming.

If you are someone who travels a great deal for work, a rabbit may not be the right pet for you, especially if you have no one to provide back-up bunny care.

Are my living circumstances right for a rabbit?

If you live in an apartment complex, or are a member of a homeowner's association, you may not be allowed to keep a pet rabbit. Find this out in advance. Beyond that, is your house laid out in such a way that you can cordon off a bunny safe room until your pet is litter trained and can have the run of the house?

Are you a renter? If so, you may not be allowed to keep a pet rabbit. Bunnies dig and chew. Your landlord is not going to be thrilled about that kind of damage.

For that matter, are you going to be all that happy when your rabbit finds a loose bit of carpet in a corner and proceeds to tunnel right under the rug?

Have you considered potential allergies?

Animal allergies are specific to species and dependent on proteins the animal excretes in some fashion, generally through saliva or urine. Just because you're allergic to cats, doesn't mean you'll be allergic to any other animal, but you may want to find out first.

Getting tested for allergies in advance is especially important if anyone in the household suffers from asthma or any other respiratory ailment.

Rabbits shed at set intervals rather than regularly as is the case with cats. You will also be dealing with their litter and bedding. If you have hay fever, you're not going to be able to tolerate using hay for your rabbit's bedding.

Will your children be a good match for a pet rabbit?

Children do quite well with rabbits, as evidenced by the popularity of showing rabbits as a 4H project. Typically children age 6 and under should not be in complete charge of a pet rabbit, and all children must be taught how to appropriately handle and interact with bunnies.

These animals are so sensitive that they can literally be frightened to death. By the same token, if a bunny is being handled poorly, they will kick and bite. On a whole, most rabbits really don't like to be held, and can respond negatively to being restrained.

Keep in mind you should avoid handling an older bunny or rabbit solely by the scruff. Not only will this practice reflect poorly on show rabbit's ability to take home a prize by making the fur look damaged, but hurts the animal when its weight is not supported by a hand under its bottom.

Do you have other pets in the household?

Rabbits can certainly co-exist with other pets, but again, you must judge the individual personality of the animals involved. Dogs and cats don't have to be able to "get at" a rabbit to frighten one to death.

Chapter 2 – Buying a Rabbit

It is certainly a very bad idea to leave a cat in unsupervised circumstances with a rabbit, especially a very small bunny.

You must also consider all the costs involved, which we will discuss in full throughout this book. They include, but are not limited to:

- the rabbit
- all the necessary equipment
- rabbit-proofing your home
- veterinary expenses

Keeping a house rabbit means some degree of altering your living arrangements and lifestyle to accommodate the bunny's habits, and emotionally investing yourself in the well-being and happiness of a living creature in need of your time, attention, and affection.

Deciding Where to Buy

While it is true that rabbits can be purchased in pet stores, you are much more likely to get a healthy rabbit from a serious hobbyist or a professional breeding operation.

Also, if you buy from someone who is a rabbit fancier, you are cultivating a relationship with a knowledgeable person who can help you by answering your questions and giving you advice as your pet matures.

It's important to try to stay away from so-called "backyard breeders." While these people may indeed love their rabbits, they are also likely seeking to make a profit, which means they will always have an eye on expenses.

Health care is often the first of those corners to be cut. There is also a good chance that the rabbits will have genetic problems if inbreeding is an issue. Many backyard breeders also house their animals outside, so the rabbit may come to you stressed or with parasites.

Serious hobbyists and breeders, on the other hand, are passionate about their bunnies and committed to raising the finest examples of the breed possible. They will belong to specialty clubs and maintain close relationships with other fanciers and experts.

Truly committed breeders participate in rabbit shows, and administer a well-thought out and active program of reproduction. Their goals are to cultivate fine bloodlines and they will protect their does from the hardships of multiple and overly frequent pregnancies. Additionally, rabbits acquired from truly passionate "rabbit people" will be better socialized, may already be trained to the litter box, and will have had proper — and documented — veterinarian care.

Finding a Healthy Rabbit

When you begin to meet perspective pet bunnies, look for all the following signs of good health:

Clear Eyes - When rabbits are healthy, they have very bright, interested eyes. There should be no sign of discharge and the overall expression should be curious and inquisitive.

Clean Ears - A rabbit that is feeling good moves its ears a lot. The ears should look and smell clean and feel velvety to the touch. There should be no discharge from the ears or excessive debris in the upper ear canal.

Healthy Fur - Bunnies should have clean fur that is thick and shiny. There should be no bald patches, and no sign that the skin is dry and flaking.

Normal Feces - Examine the area where the rabbit has been living. Make sure the feces are dry, not runny. The pills should be small and compact, with no wet appearance.

Make sure the animal you are considering is active and responds to what is going on around it. Bunnies that exhibit no interest in their environment are not healthy.

Male or Female?

Although it's a matter of some debate, most enthusiasts are in agreement that male rabbits make better pets. They tend to be more curious and interactive, and thus easier to handle.

There is the concern that male rabbits will spray. This behavior is most prevalent in young males that live in close proximity to unaltered females. Spraying is even more likely to happen if there are more than one male competing for the attention of the females or does.

Female rabbits become highly protective of their space as they reach sexual maturity. It is simply their instinct to be territorial about the area that will be their nesting place.

This can be highly confusing for owners, however, since the same doe likely started out good natured and affectionate. The real trick to having a well-behaved, loving pet of either gender is to have the animal spayed or neutered. Even the males that are not neutered may start to *court* you as the object of their affection.

One Rabbit or Two?

By nature, rabbits are happier in groups. Certainly your bunny will enjoy your companionship, but a pair of bunny pals is a sight to behold.

They will spend all their time together, and communicate via an intricate personal language. Many rabbit owners laughingly say that it looks like their bunnies are gossiping all day.

Oddly enough, having two rabbits may actually mean less work. Single bunnies get bored, lonely, and creative, which can lead to mischief.

The real deciding factor is room. If you can adequately house and care for a pair of rabbits, having two is an excellent idea.

Pros and Cons of Rabbit Ownership

As with any pet, what one person considers a positive of bunny ownership, another might consider a negative. A well-cared-for rabbit can easily live 10 years or longer.

It is absolutely imperative that you not think of a bunny as a "short-term" pet. If you are not prepared to make the same kind of commitment you would make with a dog or a cat, don't get a rabbit. In fact, although outdoor rabbits tend to live just 6-8 years, indoor house rabbits can live much longer - ranging at the high end anywhere from 12 years - and even to 16 years in rare cases! Many of the health risks outdoor rabbits are exposed to is not as much of a concern to indoor house rabbits.

Contrary to popular perception, a rabbit might not be the best pet for a child. Bunnies are not always receptive to being held, and they can bite and kick. Their unique anatomy requires that they be handled appropriately, and they must receive the proper diet, grooming, and daily care.

You will need to locate and work with a veterinarian who understands the highly specific physical ailments and diseases to which rabbits are subject. If your local vet is not knowledgeable about rabbits, you may face extra expenses, including travel, to get your pet the help it needs.

It is also necessary to bunny proof your home. While rabbits are easily trained to use a litter box, they will still chew and dig.

Spaying or neutering your pet (which is highly recommended) may reduce some of these behaviors, but it will not eliminate them entirely.

Rabbits do not just sit in their cages — especially house rabbits. At minimum, bunnies need two hours of exercise a day, and once litter-trained, should really have as much time outside of their enclosure as possible.

They are intelligent and affectionate. They don't just want interaction — they need it. For the vast majority of bunny owners, however, this is one of the great joys of living with a rabbit.

Bunnies are funny, smart, trainable, gregarious, clean, snuggly, companionable — and a whole host of other positives. They have distinct and highly individual personalities, definite likes and dislikes, and a great propensity for loyalty.

If, however, a bunny fits into your life and home and you decide to move forward, be prepared for the fact that your heart is about to be stolen.

How Much Do Rabbits Cost?

Unfortunately, that question is almost impossible to answer. Prices vary broadly depending on the breed you are buying and from whom you are making the purchase.

In general, and assuming you are not acquiring an intact animal for participation in a breeding program, you will likely pay anywhere from $20 to $300 / £12.91 to £193.61 ($21-$316 CAD)

Guide: Living with a Rabbit

Although your rabbit can't come right out and tell you what he's thinking, bunnies do have some very interesting body language as well as behavior.

- **chinning**: Any time your rabbit rubs its chin or face against a piece of furniture, a door frame, or you, he's marking the item (or person) with his scent. The message is simple. "This is mine." Even if there are no other rabbits in the household to "read" this scent marker, rabbits will do it anyway.

- **flattening out**: Wild rabbits can literally disappear from sight when they need to. When a bunny makes its body as flat as it can, he's trying not to be seen because he's afraid.

- **squatting**: Squatting is the opposite of flattening. The bunny's belly is on the floor, but he's relaxed and comfortable and his ears are up or at "half mast," not down against his head.

- **stretching out**: Rabbits, like cats, will lie on their sides and get impossibly long in the process. He doesn't have a care in the world, and he's really comfortable.

- **hopping / leaping / zooming**: Your bunny is saying, "I'm a rabbit, and I'm loving it!" Zooming bunnies are happy bunnies.

- **doing a binky**: This one is hard for new bunny owners to understand. A binky is sort of a high jump with a mid-air twist or two. It's a level of happy above zooming.

- **kicking**: You have to read the context of the situation to figure out what a bunny kick means. Exuberant kicking means the rabbit is raring and ready to go. Violent kicking means, "I have had enough" or "put me down." You'll know the difference.

- **stomping / thumping**: Basically, if your bunny gives the ground a resounding thwack with his back legs, he's giving you a warning that there's something in the environment he doesn't like. Assuming you will understand this bunny "red alert," he's letting you know what's going on.

- **sitting tall**: When a rabbit stands up on its hind legs, he's trying to get a better view of what's going on around him. The bunny may be frightened, or just curious.

- **circling**: This is a very cat-like circling of your feet, indicating the rabbit would like some love and attention, please. Don't be surprised if this turns into a case of head butting if you're rude enough to ignore your rabbit.

Any time your bunny starts shaking his ears, first check to see if those super-sensitive structures are irritated, inflamed, or smelly. This could indicate the presence of parasites. Otherwise, your rabbit is simply trying to tell you he doesn't like something — like the food you just put down, or something he's decided to smell.

Rabbits can and do bite, but if it's just a little nip, take it for what it is, a warning. What's coming next will be an honest-to-goodness chomp, and you won't like that one bit! Don't assume that a nip is coming, however. Your rabbit may just be getting ready to give you a friendly lick, which is more or less a rabbit kiss.

Rabbit Vocalizations

You may be surprised to find out that your bunny will also make a range of sounds, including purring (signaling contentment) and humming (generally only heard in intact males.)

Rabbits can also cluck, and sound amazingly chicken-like while they're doing it. You'll hear this most often at meal time when the bunny really likes whatever you've given him.

You'll also hear:

- whimpering (Stop! Leave me alone.)
- soft tooth grinding (All's well.)
- loud tooth grinding (I'm in pain.)
- hissing (Back up, buddy!)
- snorting / growling (I am ticked off!)

But the one sound you never want to hear your bunny make is a rabbit's very human-like scream indicating sheer terror.

Chapter 3 – Daily Care of Your Rabbit

Don't make the mistake of thinking that rabbits are low-maintenance pets. They take a lot of daily care. Your best bet to make this a manageable proposition for both you and the bunny is to prepare adequately in advance, get the correct equipment, and understand the fundamentals of nutrition and grooming.

Rabbit-Proofing Your Home

Don't be one of those prospective rabbit owners who laughs and says, "Why would I need to rabbit-proof my house? It's just a little bunny!" In a few days you'll be staring shell shocked at just how much damage a "little bunny" can do, or worse yet, you may be at the vet's clinic, hoping your rabbit survives whatever it got into.

Is rabbit proofing necessary? It is absolutely necessary — to protect your home, to protect your rabbit, and to make sure your bunny has everything it needs to chew naturally. Chewing is fun for rabbits. The behavior is just part of who and what they are, and they won't be happy without it.

Electrical Cables

Securing all electrical cables is the first order of business. Rabbits can be electrocuted easily or burned from biting through live electric wires. If you can't get the cables out of the reach of your rabbits, invest in a cable wrap or "tube" product.

The electrical cables are passed through the tube to create an extra secure layer between your bunny's highly efficient teeth and the dangerous wiring. The covering is typically sold in pre-measured lengths. A five-foot section (1.52 meter) retails for $6-8 US / £3.85-£5.13 UK / $6.31-$8.41 CAD.

If possible, secure cables to the base of walls with wire concealers. While this may be a time-consuming process, it is highly effective and absolutely rabbit proof. Wire concealers are available in wood grain patterns or as colored or clear plastic. Expect to pay $15-$30 US / £9.62-

£19.25 UK / $31.57 CAD for a 5 foot (1.52 meter) length of concealer.

Do NOT run your electrical cords under carpets or rugs. This can create a significant fire hazard in your home.

House and Yard Plants

Since so many house plants are toxic to rabbits, many owners opt to have no plants in the house. Even if you hang the plants from the ceiling, falling leaves can still harm your pet if consumed. It's also necessary to be vigilant about anything that might be growing in your yard or nearby garden if you take your bunny outside.

Creating a complete list of toxic plants is extremely difficult. Many that are not actually poisonous may cause severe gastrointestinal distress. The follow are all known poisons. For a more complete list, visit the Toxic and Non-Toxic Plant List maintained by the ASPCA at: http://www.aspca.org/pet-care/animal-poison-control/toxic-and-non-toxic-plants

Agave (leaves)
Amaryllis (bulbs)
Apple (seeds)
Azalea
Bird of Paradise (seeds)
Bloodroot
Buttercup (leaves)
Black Locust (seeds)

Boxwood (leaves/twigs)
Buckeye (seeds)
Buckthorn (berries)
Caladium
Calla (rhizome)
Castor Bean (seed)
Christmas Rose
Cone Flower
Crown of Thorns
Daffodil
Daphne
Delphinium
Dumbcane (Dieffenbachia)
Eggplant (plant)
Elderberry (unripe berries)
Elephant Ear
Flowering Tobacco
Foxglove
Holly (berries)
Horsechestnut (nuts)
Hyacinth
Iris
Ivy, Boston & English (berries)
Jack-in-the-Pulpit
Jerusalem Cherry
Jimson Weed
Jonquil
Lantana
Larkspur
Lily-of-the-Valley
Lupine

Mayapple
Mistletoe (berries)
Morning Glory (seeds)
Mustard (root)
Narcissus
Nicotiana
Nightshade
Oleander
Philodendron
Poison Hemlock
Poison Ivy
Potato (green)
Privet (berries)
Ranunculus
Rhododendron
Rhubarb (leaf blade)
Rosary Pea (seed)
Snow-on-the-Mountain
Sweet Pea (seeds)
Sweet Potato
Skunk Cabbage
Tansy
Tomato (leaves)
Tulip
Virginia Creeper (berries)
Water Hemlock
Wisteria (seeds/pods)
Yew (berries)

Best Indoor Habitat

Even rabbits need a place of their own. For house rabbits, that generally is an actual room, but that doesn't change the fact that a cage or hutch is an important part of keeping a pet bunny. In your mind, the hutch is a convenient place to confine your rabbit as needed.

What is better for an indoor rabbit, a cage or an indoor rabbit hutch?

Rabbit hutches are usually much larger, traditionally kept outdoors, and a mix of wood and mesh wire. Indoor rabbit hutches are a great choice if you have more than one rabbit, have a lot of space such a large basement, want to give your rabbit ample space to run in its cage especially if you can't be there to supervise a lot of necessary "bunny exercise time", or simply if you want to be able to move the hutch outdoors on occasion and don't travel a lot. Just be sure that if you are to build your own, that you do not use wood treated with harsh chemicals, as rabbits are known to gnaw on this material.

Rabbit cages, however, are more commonly used for indoor rabbits, namely due to space constraints experienced by apartment-dwellers, as well as their portability. They may be a great option for those who have time to exercise their bunny outside the cage regularly.

In selecting an indoor rabbit cage, the unit should be big enough for the rabbit to easily turn around and to stand upright without his ears touching. The absolute minimum cage or hutch dimension is four times the size of the animal that will be kept inside.

Limiting a rabbit's available space not only creates a bored, lethargic animal, but leads to rapid fouling with urine and feces. This is a very unhealthy state for the rabbit, especially if the sensitive pads on the feet become burned by the ammonia in the urine.

Cages should have enough room to accommodate a small litter box to help control this problem, and should also be able to hold a food bowl, hayrack, and water bottle. No opening in the cage should be greater than 1-2 inches (2.54 cm-5.08 cm) so the rabbit cannot catch a leg or try to stick its head through.

Look for cages with plastic slats or solid floors. Wire bottoms can hurt a rabbit's feet and cause health problems. If you have a cage with a wire bottom use a washable mat to relieve the stress. Also, select a unit that will allow the rabbit to enter through a side door, but that can be opened from the top for ease of cleaning.

Don't make the mistake of getting a cage with multiple levels. While these work well for some small animals, rabbits are strictly "on the ground" pets. They don't feel safe when raised above the ground. Go for more horizontal space, not vertical.

Bunnies do not mind cages with raised platforms, however, since most of these units are designed with ramps the rabbit can easily adapt to and feel comfortable with. Many cages take this approach to provide a clean spot for a food bowl, often on the roof of a private nesting or sleeping box.

An example of units that incorporate all of these features are the Living World Deluxe Habitats sold online at DrsFosterAndSmith.com. These cages include:

- roof access
- wire front door
- plastic base
- plastic "balcony"
- food dish that secures to the balcony
- private hiding spot
- drip proof water bottle
- hay rack
- assembles/disassembles with plastic clips
- bar spacing 1 inch / 2.54 cm

Standard
31" x 19" x 20"
(78.74 cm x 48.26 cm x 50.8 cm)
$78.99 US
£50.70 UK
$83.12 CAD

Large
38" x 22.5" x 22"
(96.52 cm x 57.15 cm x 55.88 cm)

$106.99 US
£68.66 UK
$112.60 CAD

Extra Large
47" x 23" x 24"
(119.38 cm x 58.42 cm x 60.96 cm)
$129.99 US
£83.43 UK
$136.80 CAD

Ideally, house rabbits will spend more time outside their enclosure than inside, so going with an "all in one" habitat of this type is often more cost effective.

Cage Placement

When placing the cage in your home, do not subject your rabbit to any temperature extremes. That means protecting against drafts and direct sunlight. Bunnies are very susceptible to overheating, indicative where they are completely stretched out, panting, and not eager to move - so watch for this sign.

Select an area that is well lit where your pet can observe your comings and goings. At the same time, however, make sure that your pet has time to itself and periods of peace and quiet.

Rabbits need at least eight hours of darkness per day to get enough rest, so consider covering the cage with a heavy cloth to block the light if you cannot create darkness for your pet any other way.

Definitely avoid putting the cage near either the television set or the stereo. Those big rabbit ears are sensitive and so are your pet's nerves. If you don't like a pounding stereo, imagine what it sounds like to your poor bunny!

Play Pens

Often times having a play pen for your bunny is a good idea in addition to its primary enclosure. This can help you to limit the bunny's access to parts of your home where the rabbit could do a lot of damage — or damage could be done to the rabbit!

The pens come in panels that fit together to form a "fence." They are easily taken down and put out of sight as needed. Look for a unit that is 3-4 feet / 0.9-1.21 meter high, and consider putting a hard plastic mat, carpet protector, or similar material down first to save your flooring or to provide traction for the rabbit.

A play pen that comes with a mat and a cover (should you want to set it up outside) costs approximately $75 US / £48.13 UK / $79 CAD

(Note: NEVER leave your house rabbit outdoors without supervision, even in a cage or pen.)

Basics of Nutrition

A well-rounded diet for a house rabbit should include a high-quality pellet food offered in combination with fresh hay, vegetables, and a constant supply of clean, fresh water.

Use a water bottle with a "lixit" tip rather than a water dish, which will become fouled quickly. Bottles of this type start at $10 US / £6.41 UK / $10.52 CAD

Bunnies are herbivores. Everything they eat should consist of plant matter. (See Appendix 4 for a list of suitable vegetables for your bunny.)

Pellet Foods

In assessing pellet foods, look for a formulation with no less than 18% fiber content. Pellets made from grass hay are best. Don't buy more food than you will use for your rabbit in 4-6 weeks since the pellets will go bad.

An example of a good quality pellet would be Bunny Basics Adult Rabbit Food from Oxbow Animal Health, which contains Timothy hay. The product is available in varying bag sizes:

- 5 lbs. $10 US / £6.41 UK / $10.52 CAD
- 10 lbs. $17 US / £11 UK / $17.89 CAD
- 25 lbs. $38 US / £24.38 UK / $40 CAD
- 50 lbs. $75 US / £32 UK / $79 CAD

Hay

Hay is an essential component of your pet's diet to keep the rabbit's digestive system working properly and to avoid blockages from hairballs. Wild rabbits are grazing animals, spending their days moving from plant to plant nibbling.

A captive diet that replicates this kind of variety will always make for a more healthy bunny. Young rabbits should receive primarily alfalfa. After 7 months of age, however, cut back on the alfalfa and feed a mix of Timothy, grass, oat, brome, and Bermuda hays.

Pet stores carry hay for pet rabbits, or you can go to your local feed store. Make sure the hay smells fresh, especially if you are buying an entire bale. Any moisture can lead to mold quickly.

Don't buy hay that's been sitting around for a long time. You want to get the freshest hay you can find. Never try to store more than a two-month supply and keep the hay in a location where it is out of the sun, but won't get damp.

It is imperative that you DO NOT store hay in garbage bags or any airtight container. There is moisture in the hay itself. Far from keeping the hay "safe," tightly closed methods of storage will invariably lead to mold. Storing hay in a hamper in a small apartment closet, for example, might provide a more practical and attractive option.

Daily Feeding

Your rabbit should already be weaned off its mother's milk before you bring it home. Ideally, the baby should be at least 7-12 weeks of age at adoption. From that time until age 7 months, your rabbits should receive unlimited amounts of both pellet food and hay.

As your rabbit grows, continue to leave fresh hay out at all times. At three months of age, begin introducing vegetables into your bunny's diet one item at a time in quantities no greater than half an ounce (14.175 g).

Note that all of the amounts in the following recommendations are suggestions for each 6 lbs. (2.72 kg) of body weight. If, for instance, your rabbit weighs 12 lbs. (5.44 kg), you would give double the amounts given below.

- From age 7 months to a year, feed half a cup (133 g) of pellet food per day while increasing the vegetable content of the diet. Begin to give your bunny about half an ounce of fruit a day.

- Your rabbit is considered a mature adult from 1-5 years of age. Judging on the level of activity, and the individual bunny's metabolism, feed a quarter (56.7 g) to a half a cup (133 g) of pellets a day, with at least 2 cups of chopped vegetables and 2 ounces (14.175 g) of fruit.

- For rabbits age 6 and older the regular adult diet is fine so long as your pet maintains good body weight

A twice-a-day feeding schedule works well, morning and evening, with hay and water available at all times.

Grooming

The most important aspects of grooming for a pet bunny include brushing, cleaning of the anal glands, cleaning the ears, clipping your pet's nails, and monitoring the condition of its teeth.

Shedding and Brushing

Rabbits shed every three months, generally alternating between a heavy and light episode. Bunnies are every bit as fastidious about their fur as cats, and are just as prone to developing hairballs. Unfortunately, unlike cats, they can't simply vomit up these masses.

If a rabbit is not properly groomed and these hairballs are allowed to form, they can lead to stomach blockages that will cause the animal to starve. Weekly brushings to get rid of loose hair during the "off season" are a must. During a heavy shedding period, brush your bunny several times a day.

Some rabbits will shed for two weeks before they have gotten rid of their old fur, while others can be done in as little as 24 hours. It's not at all unusual to be able to remove large handfuls of hair from your pet when it is shedding. If mats form, do not cut them out with scissors. You could seriously injure your pet.

Use your fingers to very gently tease the mats apart. Hold the mat at the base so the skin does not get pulled, and work slowly to remove the tangled hair.

Bald spots are common while bunnies are shedding, and are not anything to be concerned about. The hair will grow back quickly.

(Note that bunnies with longer hair will need to be brushed more frequently, especially when they are shedding, to prevent mats and tangles.)

Any small animal "slicker" brush will work well with a bunny, remembering to always take care not to damage the animal's skin. Brushes with pliable plastic teeth outfitted with soft tips are gentle on the skin, but do a good job of removing loose hair. Expect to pay around $5 US / £3.2 UK / $5.26 CAD

Bathing

As for baths, rabbits can swim if they have to, but they dislike being wet as much or more than most breeds of cats. Getting wet is, in fact, very dangerous for rabbits since hypothermia can set in quickly.

If your rabbit does get wet, never blow dry your pet on anything more than the "warm" setting. Bunnies have delicate skin and can be burned easily.

Always monitor the temperature of the animal's skin with your hand and place your hand in the path of the blow dryer to disperse the most direct flow of air.

Anal Glands

Rabbits have two sets of scent glands. One is located under their chin and is used for marking items — and humans — as their own. The second set is located on either side of the animal's genitals.

The anal glands are subject to building up a brown, oily, and very smelly substance that must be cleaned. Use a cotton swab dipped in warm water. Hold your bunny gently but securely, and carefully clean away the brown matter.

The process does not take long, and should be performed regularly.

Feet and Nails

Because they live inside and do not naturally wear down their toenails, house rabbits will need the occasional pedicure. Use the same kind of clippers you would use for a dog and cat. Expect to perform this chore every 6-8 weeks.

Trim only the white portion of the nail. If you nick the vascular quick, you will hurt your bunny and cause a profuse amount of bleeding that may take some time to stop.

Any standard small animal nail clipper will work well for this task. It's best, however, to get a clipper designed for use with pets rather than use human clippers.

Clippers for animals are sharper, and tend to be designed after the fashion of pliers, which will give you a steadier grip on the implement, especially if your bunny is protesting its pedicure.

Expect to pay from $10 to $30 US (£6.41-£19.25 UK / $10.51-$31.57 CAD)

Pay attention to the condition of the fur on the bottom of the feet, which serves as padding. If the pads look inflamed or if callouses are forming, you need to provide more rugs and resting mats for your rabbit.

Any exposed skin on the feet can be easily burned by rabbit urine and become subject to infection.

Any time your bunny is experiencing problems with its feet, be extra vigilant about cleaning the litter box and cage daily. Both must be kept clean and dry.

Ears

Wax can build up in your rabbit's ears and must be gently cleaned out with a cotton swab. Be very cautious not to push the wax farther down in the ear canal.

If your bunny's ears have a strong, yeasty odor, or are unusually dirty and filled with debris, your pet likely has a case of ear mites. Consult your veterinarian and get an appropriate cleaner and topical medication.

Teeth

Your rabbit's teeth will never stop growing. It's important to monitor your pet's teeth to make sure they are being worn down properly through chewing and gnawing.

If the teeth overgrow, they can prevent the rabbit from eating well. A bunny's teeth can be clipped, but many owners balk at this chore. A veterinarian can clip your rabbit's teeth for you, but you must monitor this aspect of your pet's health and grooming regularly.

Always make sure your bunny has adequate chew toys. This is an essential of good bunny care.

An example would be Oxbow Timothy Club Carrot & Twists, which is an edible chew toy that is a source of both fiber and entertainment. These items cost $3-$5 US / £2-£3.2 UK / $3-$5 CAD

Leash Training

Under ideal conditions, leash training for a rabbit should begin early in your pet's life. You will want to select a lightweight harness. Collars are out of the question. Bunnies can slip right out of them, and likely harm themselves in the process as rabbit necks and spines are not designed for them to be effective.

Schools of thought are divided on the best type of harness. Many owners prefer a simple unit with two straps, one that passes around the chest behind the front lets and another that goes down over the neck. The point of attachment for the lead is between the shoulder blades.

This type of harness costs under $10 US / £6.45 UK / $10.53 CAD.

The principle objection against these harnesses is the pressure they can place on the animal's neck. The second type of harness is, for all practical purposes a vest. This places the lead point farther down the back, and puts no strain on the animal's neck whatsoever.

Harnesses of this type retail for $10-$20 US / £6.45-£13 UK / $10.53-$21 CAD.

The first time you put the harness on your rabbit, hold your pet gently but firmly. Don't try to put the rabbit in your lap. Fit the harness in place with your rabbit on the floor. Make sure the harness fits snug for safety, neither too tight on loose, only allowing two of your fingers between the rabbit's body and the harness.

Speak softly and soothingly to your pet and offer it treats every time it's cooperative. You may have to spend several days just getting the bunny used to having the harness put in place. Let the rabbit wear the harness for a few minutes and then remove it.
When you first attach the leash, let the bunny just drag it along behind him. The rabbit needs to get used to the feeling of the harness moving with its body, and to the slight extra weight of the lead.

Take the first few "walks" indoors. For the most part, all you're going to be doing is following the rabbit around. The important thing is that you have control of the situation in case the rabbit panics.

You can entice the rabbit to move in the direction you want by offering treats and using the usual types of "command" words and phrases like, "come on" or "let's go."

Even if your bunny never takes well to going out on a leash, it's important to get your pet used to the harness and lead.

When you transport your rabbit, it should always be in an appropriately fastened pet carrier, but if there is any chance at all that your bunny will panic and bolt, the harness and leash are an important extra precaution.

Litter Box Training

It's much easier to litter box train a rabbit than most people realize because bunnies routinely pick one or more spots to urinate and deposit their pellets. (This is often a corner.) If you simply place their box in an area the rabbit has already selected, they will use it.

Young rabbits do not have a long attention span, however, so it may take a while for a little bunny to get the hang of things. Older rabbits, however, are much easier to train, as are animals that have been spayed or neutered.

At age 4-6 months rabbits sexually mature and begin to mark their territory. Once they've been "fixed" they are more likely to settle down and use their box.

Types of Litter

Rabbits have a tendency to spend a lot of time in their litter boxes, and they will nibble on whatever litter you use. Pick a litter that is not only safe for your pet, but that is easy for you to change, since rabbit urine is pungent and strong. Daily maintenance is a must. To ensure your rabbit is happiest, it's best to also get as large of a box as you can since bunnies love to frolic there as well.

Bunnies will use clay litter, but if your rabbit is a digger, it will create a real dust cloud. This isn't just an issue of a mess for you. The dust weakens your rabbit's lungs, and raises the potential for your pet to contract pneumonia. Also, clay litter clumping can pose a health risk to nibbly bunny types by creating an intestinal blockage.

Organic litters made of some combination of citrus, oat, alfalfa, or paper, are good choices. Don't use soft wood litters that contain shavings or chips, like pine or cedar. These products give off gases that have been linked to liver damage in rabbits. Also avoid any newspaper little that has ink dyes that could be toxic.

Avoid the product Swheat Scoop Litter since it's not good for bunnies. It's made of wheat, which rabbits will eat. The high carbohydrate content of wheat leads to obesity, as well as increased cecal production and diarrhea. There are similar problems with corn cob litters that will cause intestinal blockages.

Many owners opt to line the bottom of the litter box with newspaper and then use a handful of hay, which encourages good litter box habits because the rabbits enjoy nibbling on it.

The newspaper absorbs the urine to draw it away from the animal and keep the hay drier, but it doesn't help with odor control. Make sure the newspapers you're using have been printed with soy-based ink to avoid any toxicity for your pet.

Unique Rabbit Digestion

Rabbits have a unique digestive system that actually produces two kinds of pellets. The feces you will typically see in the litter box are dry and round.

The second type of droppings are called cecum and are often referred to as "night droppings," although the time of day when a rabbit will expel them varies.

The cecal pellets or cecatropes will be re-ingested by the bunny so your pet can benefit from the essential nutrients created in a part of its digestive tract called the cecum.

There, bacteria and fungi partially digest food and essentially "process" it for optimum value for the rabbit. Cecal pellets are small and brown, and look something like a tiny bunch of grapes. They have a slightly pungent odor.

You may occasionally see one of these pellets in your rabbit's box, but since the bunny's system signals the rabbit when the pellets are ready to be excreted, they are normally consumed immediately.

Litter Recommendations

Litter products that consistently get good reviews from rabbit owners include:

Carefresh Litter Plus Premium Small Animal Litter

This product is a highly absorbent blend of low-dust pellets with a good reputation for odor control.

It does not tend to clump, or stick to the bottom of the box. Carefresh is both biodegradable and compostable.

Cost - $10 US / £6.41 UK / $10.52 CAD for 16.5 lbs. / 7.5 kg

Cat Country

Cat Country is manufactured from Western Red Winter Wheat Grass that bond to urine preventing the formation of ammonia.

The product is organic, and contains no chemicals.

Cost - $15 US / £9.62 UK / $15.78 CAD for 20 lbs. / 9 kg

Critter Country

Critter Country is sold as small animal bedding, but can also be used as a litter. It is also made of Harvested Winter Wheatgrass for superior odor control and absorbency.

Cost - $27 US / £17.32 UK / $28.41 CAD for 20 lbs. / 9 kg

Purina Yesterday's News Paper-Based Crumble Cat Litter

This product is non-toxic and designed to absorb three-times as much moisture as clay. The texture is soft, and there are no added chemicals.

Cost - $17 US / £11 UK / $17.89 CAD for 26 lbs. / 11.8 kg

PaPurr Scoopable Cat Litter

Also non-toxic and completely biodegradeable, PaPurr is suitable for all small animals. It has the consistency of clay with much greater absorbent qualities.

Cost - $38 US / £24.38 UK / $40 CAD for 18 lbs. / 8.16 kg

Rabbits don't tend to be as particular about the texture of their litter as cats. The important points in your selection are to find something that fits your budget that is non-toxic, will not harm your rabbit if eaten and that has high absorbency and odor control.

Cleaning the Litter Box

Chapter 3 – Daily Care of Your Rabbit

Like most small animals, rabbits far prefer to have a clean box. Keep all household chemicals away from your pets. Use white vinegar to rinse your rabbit's pans, letting them soak to remove any tough stains.

For accidents that occur outside the litter pan, clean up with a mixture of white vinegar or club soda. Dried urine can be more problematic, but products like Nature's Miracle Stain & Odor Remover are highly effective. A 24 oz. / 0.7 liter bottle sells for approximately $10 US / £6.41 UK / $10.52 CAD.

For more serious stains, try Nature's Miracle Urine Destroyer, which uses bio-enzymatic ingredients to penetrate difficult surfaces like carpets. This product works especially well if your rabbit has been "using" a new favorite spot that you do not detect for several days. (37 oz. / 1.09 liter $16 US / £10.26 UK / $16.83 CAD)

Guide: Estimated Costs:

The following are the estimated costs for acquiring a rabbit and the initial necessary supplies. Of course many costs, like food and chew toys are an on-going expense and must be considered on a monthly basis.

Rabbit

Varies widely by breed and source.

$20 - $300 US
£12.91 - £193.61 UK
$21 - $316 CAD

Rabbit Proofing

Costs vary depending on your approach to this important task. Budget $100 to $150 for items like cord minders and concealers, as exposed electrical cables are a major hazard that must be addressed.

Habitat

Assuming you begin with a habitat designed for a rabbit and sold as a "kit" with items like food / water bowls and hay rack included: $80 - $150

Guide: Estimated Costs:

Play Pen

Depending on size and assuming mats and covers are included: $75 - $100

Pellet Foods

5-50 lbs. - $10-$75

Fresh Foods

The cost of hay, fresh fruits, and vegetables varies widely by source and amount.

Grooming

Brush $5 US / £3.2 UK / $5.26 CAD
nail clipper $10 to $30 US (£6.41-£19.25 UK / $10.51-$31.57 CAD)

Chew Toys

Varies widely, but expect per toy to pay $3-$5 US / £2-£3.2 UK / $3-$5 CAD.

Harness

Varies by style, $10-$20 US / £6.45-£13 UK / $10.53-$21 CAD

Guide: Estimated Costs:

Litter

Varies by type and volume, $10-$40 US / £6.45-£25.67 UK / $10.53-$42 CAD

Stain and Odor Removers

Nature's Miracle Stain & Odor Remover
24 oz. / 0.7 liter bottle
$10 US / £6.41 UK / $10.52 CAD

Nature's Miracle Urine Destroyer
37 oz. / 1.09 liter bottle
$16 US / £10.26 UK / $16.83 CAD

Total Estimate:

$350 - $875 US
£225 - £562 UK
$368 - $921 CAD

Chapter 4 – Rabbit Health

One of the most important things any rabbit owner can understand is that your bunny will not tell you when it's ill. Nature tells the bunny to appear as healthy as possible. Rabbits that seem sick or weak wind up being prey for larger animals.

The best preventive medicine your rabbit will ever have is a vigilant owner who is aware of signs of illness. In fact, keeping your bunny indoors may allow you the advantage to better monitor its health by keeping a closer eye on its behavior changes and symptoms than if it was raised outdoors. You will need a good veterinarian partner in

keeping your bunny healthy. Finding the right vet —
possibly even before you adopt a rabbit — is the first step
in your pet's long-term healthcare plan.

(*Note*: Many illnesses and conditions in rabbits manifest
with hind limb weakness or paralysis. Always take your
bunny to the vet at the first sign of problems with the hind
legs.)

Finding a Rabbit Vet

Never wait until you are faced with a healthcare crisis to
find a veterinarian to treat your bunny. It may seem an
obvious statement, but rabbits aren't like cats and dogs —
literally. Bunnies have a unique physiology that most small
animal vets don't understand.

Rabbits fall into the category of "exotics" for their medical
needs. Vets who specialize in the treatment of less common
companion animals typically list themselves as exotic
specialists. This should mean that the vet has both special
training and experience with the species they treat.

Ideally, you want to find a vet that is skilled at handling,
diagnosing, and treating your rabbit while using a good
bedside manner to deal with you.

This can be a daunting set of criteria for people living in
rural areas who have no choice but to deal with small
animal vets, or with those that deal primarily work with
large animals and livestock.

If this is your situation, you will be in a position of being your bunny's advocate. You may well understand more about your pet than the vet, and you will have to be willing to step up and ask for tests or treatments that are appropriate for a rabbit.

Be prepared, in severe cases, to travel to a larger town or city where you can get the specialized treatment your pet may require.

There are many ways to locate a veterinarian that works with rabbits, starting with personal referrals from other rabbit owners. You can also consult the state-by-state list of recommended vets maintained by the House Rabbit Society at www.rabbit.org/vets/vets.html

The Association of Exotic Mammal Veterinarians at aemv.org is also a valuable resource, as is your local rabbit breed club or 4H club.

Interviewing a Prospective Vet

When you have a short list of potential vets, call the clinic and ask some questions. You want someone who has been treating rabbits two years or longer and, ideally, has special training with rabbits.

Find out how many bunnies are treated at the practice per week, and how many rabbits are spayed or neutered there each month. Additionally, find out what antibiotics are typically used on rabbits, as some of the medicines routinely prescribed to cats and dogs are potentially fatal to bunnies.

What is the arrangement at the clinic for after-hours emergencies? If you and your bunny are to be sent to an emergency clinic, what degree of experience does that facility have with rabbits?

Ask to come to the clinic to see the facility and meet the staff. There should be no reluctance on the part of the vet to allow such a visit, but expect to make an appointment so that your presence does not disrupt the treatment of other patients. You are looking for a clean clinic with friendly, knowledgeable personnel.

If you are sufficiently impressed with the doctor and the clinic to consider using their services, inquire about a schedule of fees to make sure you can afford to use the vet in question. Understand that veterinarian care is not cheap, and generally exotic animal vets charge higher fees.

Spaying and Neutering

Spaying and neutering will not only prevent the proliferation of more unwanted rabbits in the world but it will also improve your pet's behavior and overall health.

Rabbits that have been spayed or neutered tend to live longer than intact animals and to suffer from fewer diseases.

Intact male rabbits are prone to spraying strong smelling urine and to engage in other problem behaviors such as "courting" their owners if there isn't another appropriate object for their affections. For females, spaying reduces incidents of uterine cancer and other serious reproductive conditions including, but not limited to:

- false pregnancies
- mammary gland disorders
- pregnancy toxemia
- endometriosis
- pyometra (accumulations of pus in the uterus)
- uterine adenocarcinoma
- uterine aneurysm

Rabbits reach sexual maturity at age 4 months or later. At that time, either procedure may be performed, but females should be spayed before 2 years of age to get the full health benefits of the procedure.

For vets with experience treating rabbits, the spaying and neutering procedures are routine. Owners should not be concerned about the need for anesthesia in these cases.

Rabbits tolerate both anesthetic gas and injectables quite well, and even with routine diagnostic procedures, it's often better to sedate the rabbits to minimize stress.

The costs for spaying and neutering will vary by location and vet, and will be affected by your pet's age and overall health. Since the spaying procedure does require abdominal surgery, it is generally twice the cost of neutering. Also, many vets require pre-surgical lab work as a precaution.

Urinary Tract Health

Rabbits are prone to a number of kidney and bladder ailments, all requiring treatment by a veterinarian. Monitor your pet's urine for any changes in color. Normal bunny urine can range from a light yellow to deep orange. This is a consequence of either pigments from food, or natural porphyrines excreted by the bladder.

Although it can be difficult to tell, you must be on the watch for urine that is bright red or streaked with red indicating the presence of blood. If this is present in an intact doe, it can be coming from the reproductive tract. Regardless, however, if there is any sign of blood in the urine, your pet must be examined by a vet immediately.

The problem could be a case of cystitis or something more serious like a urinary tract or bladder infection. Also watch for small amounts of urine outside of the area where the bunny normally "goes."

Rabbits with urinary tract problems may also pass small stones. They will exhibit depressed behaviour, and may hunch up indicating the presence of abdominal pain.

Bacteria, parasites, toxins, and cancers can lead to renal or kidney disease in rabbits. Bunnies with renal problems will be anemic, evident by pale gums, a depressed mood, poor appetite, and weight loss. They will produce excessive amounts of urine and drink a lot of water.

The best prevention for any kind of urinary problem in pet rabbits is to make sure they have a constant supply of clean, fresh water and are fed a healthy diet including moisture-rich fresh foods.

Also, keeping their toilet area clean will encourage urination. Bunnies that don't like the condition of their litter box have a tendency to "hold it." Finally, make sure your rabbit is getting enough physical exercise.

Dental Disease

As stated before, because a rabbit's teeth never stop growing, dental disease and tooth-related problems are quite common. If a rabbit's teeth are improperly misaligned, they won't wear down properly. If the teeth grow too long, the rabbit can't chew. Either case affects the degree of nutrition the bunny is getting on a daily basis.

Either the crown or the root of a tooth can overgrow. In the case of the crown, the resulting sharp edges will cause sores in the mouth and on the tongue.

Overgrown roots lead to jaw deformities and ultimately to abscesses. If the roots of the upper incisors overgrow, they can even block the tear ducts, leading to chronic tear production.

The most common cause of dental problems in pet rabbits is a lack of adequate abrasive material in the diet. Issues with the teeth can, however, also be an early sign of metabolic bone disease or even a result of genetic flaws and inbreeding.

Symptoms of dental disease in bunnies include picky eating and the inability to consume anything hard, including pellets and tougher, root vegetables. The rabbit's eyes may bulge. It will drop its food often and salivate excessively. The appetite will decline, and there may be discharge from both the eyes and nose.

Tooth grinding is likely, and there may be lumps along the jaw or in the area under the eye. At the sign of any of these symptoms, it is imperative that you get your pet to the veterinarian. In its early stages, dental disease may not exhibit any outward signs, so a thorough oral exam during the rabbit's annual checkup is a crucial aspect of preventive healthcare.

Abscesses

Abscesses are not exclusively a dental issue. They can occur anywhere on the body, and present as a pocket of dense pus in a region of inflamed tissue. The infection is typically caused by bacteria, and may be the result of a bite or puncture, dental disease, or a broader systemic infection.

Draining the area is difficult, so that completely removing the affected tissue is one of the most common treatments, although the viability of this option varies greatly by location. It is also important that the vet find and address the underlying cause.

Any unusual lumps on your rabbit must be evaluated immediately by your veterinarian. Such masses may indicate the presence of an abscess, or they could be tumors or cysts.

Ear Infections

Obviously a rabbit's ears are one of its most prominent features, and an area of the body prone to developing yeast infections and to suffer from mite infestations. If untreated, such issues can lead to "head tilt". This is especially prevalent in breeds with lop ears where the warm, moist setting is prime for the growth of bacteria.

If your bunny is scratching its ears, seems reluctant for you to touch the ears, and has runny eyes, it needs to be examined by a veterinarian.

A strong yeasty smell and the presence of black, tarry debris in excess in the ear are also key signs of mite infestation and possible infection.

Torticollis

Torticollis or head tilt can be caused by any one of a number of issues including, but not limited to inner ear disease, a vestibular disorder, cancer, trauma, stroke, or a parasitic infection.

Any time your bunny is tilting its head to one side constantly, it must be assessed by the vet. Head tilt can often be corrected if the underlying problem is treated, but there are instances in which the tilt is permanent.

If the torticollis is irreversible, but your bunny is still active, eating well, and seeming to enjoy life, there is no reason why the rabbit cannot live with the condition. He'll just have a slightly different view of the world!

Inflammation of the Feet

Like the oversized ears, a rabbit's big hind feet are subject
to problems, including pododermatitis or sore hocks, which
strikes the joint closest to the paw on the high leg. This
region becomes inflamed easily, with resulting hair loss and
the potential for painful ulcers to develop.

Sore hocks can be caused by a bacterial infection, obesity, a
dirty and wet cage, or limited space to take exercise. The
wound must be cleaned and treated with an antibiotic, and
the underlying cause of the irritation must be identified and
corrected.

This may mean your rabbit needs to lose weight, you need to buy a bigger cage, or the animal needs more time outside the enclosure to play and move around. If you are housing your rabbit in a cage or hutch with a wire floor, provide more mats or rugs to give your pet a resting spot with cushioning away from the wire.

Obesity

Just as is the case in humans, being overweight increases your rabbit's risk of developing a broad range of other health problems.

All companion rabbits need to be fed a properly balanced diet, and your pet should be weighed regularly to monitor its body mass.

Rabbits that are overweight will have difficulty grooming, are more prone to inflammation of the feet, and may not be able to ingest their own cecatropes.

The digestive tract becomes sluggish and unhealthy in obese bunnies, and in general their lifespan is considerably shortened. Their hearts suffer from the stress, and they may have mobility issues due to the strain on their vertebrae.

A prime cause of obesity in bunnies is the use of pellet foods that have too much alfalfa in the ingredient list. In order to keep your bunny at a healthy weight, feed more hay and fresh foods, and fewer pellets.

Common Parasites

There are a number of parasites with which pet rabbits may become infested. These include intestinal and ear parasites, as well as those that affect other organs, the fur, and skin.

Intestinal

Common intestinal parasites include roundworms, pinworms, protozoa, and tapeworms. Signs of their presence in your bunny's system include a distended abdomen and a dry, unhealthy coat.

You may also see signs of worms in the litter box and near the anus. Rabbits with parasites will lose weight even though they are eating well.

A fecal sample is required to confirm the presence and to identify the type of intestinal parasite plaguing your rabbit. Treatment will be either an oral or injectable deworming agent.

In order to cut down on the risk of your pet developing internal parasites, avoid letting your bunny graze in areas outside where wild rabbits may have been present, or where dogs and cats have defecated.

Ear Mites

Ear mites cause extreme itchiness. Your bunny will shake its head and scratch in an effort to relieve its discomfort.

Inside the ear you'll be able to see a dark, crusty discharge and the area will smell foul.

Separate the affected bunny from any others in the home as mites are highly contagious.

The vet will need to examine the discharge under a microscope to determine the appropriate treatment, which will likely be a thorough cleaning of the ear following by the application of a topical agent for several days to two weeks.

The mites that affect rabbits are different than those from which cats suffer, but cats can carry the parasite that will infect rabbits.

Fur Mites

Fur mites are often called "walking dandruff." These tiny, spider-like pests create dry, flaking skin and, if untreated, red, crusty patches will appear on the rabbit's spine and rump. In severe instances, the bunny will lose clumps of its hair.

Often the same treatments are used for fur mites as those recommended for fleas, but consult your veterinarian. A thorough cleaning of the rabbit's bedding and enclosure is also recommended.

Fleas

Rabbits are just as susceptible to flea infestations as dogs or cats, and are treated with the same kinds of topical applications. It is important, however, that you do not resort to commercially available powders, dips, or shampoos. Many of these products are toxic to bunnies and can cause fatal reactions.

In seeking treatment from your vet for the problem, you will likely be advised to use Advantage, Program, or Revolution. (Never use Frontline for dogs on rabbits.)

Although these remedies are generally accepted as safe solutions that will keep your pet flea free for months at a time, a word of caution is in order.

All of these products contain pyrethrum and have come under fire from users whose pets have suffered a range of negative reactions, from permanent nerve damage to death.

This has been particularly true in small dog breeds and in cats. Consumers and animal advocates continue to call for the removal of these products from the market.

There are natural alternatives to flea control, and in all cases, a thorough washing and disinfecting of all bedding and of the immediate area is in order, especially if you have carpet. Discuss these options with your vet, and with other rabbit enthusiasts online. Natural products can also be toxic.

Fleas are a nuisance, and are certainly not healthy for your rabbit, but in this case, it is possible for the cure to be much worse. Proceed with caution.

Flies

While common flies are not a problem for most companion animals, these pests do like to lay their eggs around a rabbit's rectal area, especially if the region is moist and dirty.

In truth, flies will exploit any compromised area of the body, especially cuts or open sores. When the eggs hatch, the maggots burrow deeply into the wound feeding on the flesh.

It is important to ensure that your rabbit's rectal area is kept clean at all times, especially if the bunny spends any time in an outside enclosure or has long hair. It is very easy for feces to become trapped under the tail and attract flies.

In treating the area, your vet will need to remove all the fly eggs and maggots, as well as the surrounding dead tissue and then prescribe the appropriate treatments.

Encephalitozoonosis

This condition is caused by the parasite *Encephalitozoon cuniculi*, which is shed through the urine and then passed to other rabbits. Nursing does frequently transmit the disease to their babies through the placenta, or during weaning.

Encephalitozoonosis affects virtually the entire system, but is particularly damaging to the brain, spinal cord, kidney, and heart. The symptoms include head tilt, overall clumsiness, and a wobbling gait or a complete inability to use the hind legs.

The condition is hard to diagnose, and there is no cure. Thankfully, many rabbits that are exposed to the parasite never become symptomatic, but the disease is fatal.

Baylisascaris

This round worm is transmitted through raccoon feces and is most prevalent in bunnies that have access to the outdoors, including decks and patios. The parasite is also often found in contaminated hay.

Once in the body, baylisascaris migrates widely and also travels to the brain. It causes both inflammation and tissue damage.

The symptoms include head tilt, blindness, loss of coordination, abdominal pain, partial or full paralysis, sudden lethargy, coma, and sudden death.

Standard de-wormers will rid the intestine of the adult form of the parasite, but there is no known treatment for the migrating larva, and the condition is generally fatal. If the rabbit does survive, it can exhibit marked disability and behavioral changes.

The parasite is also harmful, and potentially deadly to humans as well.

Other Health Issues

Some of the other conditions to which bunnies are subject are discussed below. They vary in severity, but always take one rule of thumb as your standard: bunnies are sensitive creatures, if something is wrong, consult your vet.

Upper Respiratory Disease

Rabbits, like other pets — and like humans — frequently develop the equivalent of the common cold. In bunnies, respiratory infections are referred to as the "snuffle."

Symptoms include sneezing, runny nose, and matted fur inside the front legs. (Bunnies essentially wipe their noses on their sleeves!)

The rabbit's breathing may be labored. It will be in a lethargic, depressed state, and probably disinterested in food. The bunny may tilt or shake its head.

Respiratory infections are typically caused by the bacteria, *bordatella bronchiseptica* and *pasteurellamultocid*, the same agents that cause kennel cough in dogs.

This is a nuisance condition, treated with palliative care, and will resolve in two to three weeks on its own.

Ringworm

Ringworm is not all that prevalent in rabbits, but it does occur in multi-pet households where your bunny is exposed to other animals, like cats, that do contract ringworm more easily.

The dry, crusty lesions are caused by one of several types of fungi, and are caused when the rabbit comes into contact with the spores. Consult your vet for the correct topical agents to cure the outbreak.

Myxomatosis

Myxomatosis is transmitted by insects and is caused by several strains of the pox virus. It is so deadly to rabbits that it was intentionally spread among wild populations in Europe in the 19th century to control the spread of the animals and stop their depredations on agricultural crops.

Thankfully, the version seen in the United States is milder than the European sprain, but this is still a serious illness that in its severe form is fatal.

Your rabbit will be lethargic and run a fever. The eyes will be watery, red and swollen, and the genitals will also become inflamed and enlarged. In the final stage facial swelling will occur.Always take your rabbit to the vet immediately if you suspect a case of myxomatosis.

Tyzzer's Disease

Tyzzer's Disease is caused by a bacteria, and can be fatal in young rabbits that have just been weaned and in older bunnies, who develop chronic wasting disease as a result.

The bacteria typically strikes rabbits who are fed a low fiber diet with high carbohydrates and who are subject to poor hygiene. The rabbit will exhibit a depressed state and suffer from watery, profuse diarrhea.

There is no recommended treatment beyond supportive care in the hope that the condition resolves itself.

Venereal Disease

Venereal disease in rabbits, as in all species subject to these infections, are spread by sexual contact. Rabbits contract a form of syphilis. Preventing this disease is another compelling reason to spay and neuter your rabbits.

Rabbits with syphilis will suffer from crusty sores on their genitals, as well as on the lips, nose, chin, and eyelids.The condition is curable with injections of penicillin.

Viral Hemorrhagic Disease

Viral Hemorrhagic Diseaseis a deadly condition first seen in rabbits in Europe in 1988 and in the United States in 2000. It is caused by the *Calici* virus.

It is transmitted by oral contact with contaminated feces. All major organs are affected, and rabbits die within days.

Not all rabbits who are exposed come down with the condition, but in those that do, the disease is 100% fatal.

Symptoms include a high fever, lethargy, loss of appetite, spasms, and spontaneous bleeding from the mouth and rectum followed by sudden death. Veterinarians are required to report outbreaks of the disease to the proper authorities.

The best prevention is to keep an affected rabbit away from other bunnies. If the disease is present in your area do not use grooming tools, cages, or other implements other rabbits have used. Two cages is also recommended in this case.

Always wash your hands after handling unfamiliar rabbits at shows, in shelters, or in another rabbitry.

A Word on Antibiotics

The use of oral amoxicillin can be fatal to rabbits. The drug destroys the healthy bacteria in the gastrointestinal tract, which can lead to enteritis.

There are many safe antibiotics that can be used with rabbits, but you must make sure that you are working with a vet experienced in caring for bunnies.

Always ask about this issue before allowing your rabbit to receive any antibiotic orally, via an injection, or as a topical agent.

Elderly Bunnies

Any rabbit aged 10 years or older is considered to be a senior citizen. Obviously the better care the rabbit receives, the healthier it will be. Some issues commonly seen in older bunnies include:

- kidney problems
- arthritis
- sore hocks
- hind leg weakness or paralysis
- dental disease
- blindness
- deafness
- cancer

You may find that it will be necessary to make adaptations so that your older rabbit can have an easier, more enjoyable life. These measures might include cutting down one side of the litter box for better access and lowering both the hay rack and the water bottle.

Make sure older bunnies have soft places to sit and always monitor their hocks for callouses and open sores. Give them non-skid surfaces to accommodate arthritic joints and to reduce stress, and ensure they stay good and warm.

Preventive Health Care

You are your bunny's best preventive health care plan. The best thing you can do for your pet after finding an appropriate veterinarian is to have the rabbit spayed or neutered. This alone will eliminate a huge degree of health risk.

The next major component is good nutrition with an emphasis not just on pellet foods, but on fresh vegetables with some fruit, plenty of hay, and lots and lots of clean water. Tough abrasive root vegetables will keep your rabbit's teeth worn down, and hay will keep its digestive tract working well.

As you are cleaning your rabbit's cage and the area surrounding it, be on watch for anything out of the ordinary in your pet's urine or feces.

Handle your bunny and observe its eyes, nose, feet, and mouth. If you think something is wrong, it probably is. Never hesitate to consult your veterinarian.

Finally, make sure your rabbit has an annual wellness exam. There are many illness that you won't see until serious symptoms manifest but that your vet can detect early and treat before your bunny's overall health is put at risk.

Breeding Rabbits

For the hobbyist and pet owner, the answer to breeding rabbits is a resounding, "No." There are far too many unwanted rabbits in the world, especially in the wake of the Easter holidays when shelters are inundated with young rabbits that were given as gifts and then judged to be too much trouble.

If you want more than one bunny, consider adopting one from a shelter. If you truly want to breed rabbits, and have the room — and the time to do the normal maintenance routines times the number of bunnies — then your best bet is to find an existing breeder who will serve as your mentor.

There are too many ins and outs of breeding for the scope of this book to adequately cover the entire process of establishing a rabbitry. The mechanics of it all are not difficult. Rabbits reach sexual maturity at 4 months of age and left to their own devices, they will reproduce prolifically.

However, care must be taken not to subject does to the stresses of multiple pregnancies. There are many "female" problems (discussed in the chapter on health) that can significantly shorten a rabbit's lifespan.

Intact male rabbits have a tendency to spray strong urine, and both genders can become quite aggressive.

Do not proceed with a breeding program until you have investigated the proposition fully.

Guide: Showing Rabbits

Although many 4-H members show rabbits as their club project, people of all ages are involved in rabbit shows associated with a variety of venues including fairs and livestock shows.

Below is a general overview of the process. You will need to do your research in advance and understand exactly what is required for your rabbit to conform to the highest show standards for its breed and class.

Finding a Show

To locate a directory of rabbit shows, start with the governing body for your areas. For instance:

- American Rabbit Breeders Association at www.arba.net

- The British Rabbit Council at www.thebrc.org

- The Dominion and Cavy Breeders Association (Canada) at www.drcba.ca

Contact the show organizers for a catalog containing all the information you'll need:
- location
- start times (check in and show by breed)
- entry fees
- judging
- rules

Be prepared to fill out an entry form and to submit a full or partial pre-entry fee. (Some shows allow you to pay the fee and do all the paperwork on the "day of entry.")

If for any reason your stated entry cannot participate in the show and you "scratch" that rabbit, one of the same breed, gender, and class can normally be substituted.

The Day of the Show

The official in charge of the show (a superintendent or a show committee) will assemble a list of breeds in the order in which they will be judged. Normally, the breed with the largest number of entries go first.

You will be assigned an area in the hall to wait with your caged rabbit(s) until you are called for judging. Watch the time, and make sure your rabbit is groomed just before his turn at the judging table.

See Appendix 1 for American Rabbit Breeder's Association Show Standard and Appendix 2 for The British Rabbit Council Breed Standards. These documents and the links they provide will help you to understand the basics of showmanship for your particular breed.

Afterword

Hopefully by now you have come to realize that having a house rabbit does not mean you have a bunny living in a cage inside. Certainly a companion rabbit's cage is his den, but at minimum, your rabbit needs 2 hours of exercise a day -- preferably in a rabbit-safe room or rooms.

House rabbits are not low-maintenance pets. Their housekeeping will eat up about an hour of your time a day, but in exchange, you will welcome an intelligent, curious, affectionate, and fun creature into your life.

Most people are surprised to learn how easily rabbits can be trained to use a litter box, and even more surprised at just how much "rabbit proofing" they have to do to get ahead of the chewing and the digging. These behaviors are not evidence of a bunny gone bad, but rather a rabbit being a rabbit.

You should never bring a bunny or any other kind of companion animal into your life until you know exactly what to expect -- and what is expected of you. All pets deserve the best care they can possibly receive including proper veterinary services. With rabbits, this may be challenging as technically they are classed as "exotics."

Not every vet is going to know how to take care of rabbit-specific ailments, of which there are many. Thankfully, however, if you have your pet spayed or neutered -- which is highly recommended -- the risk of many of these illnesses drops significantly. Keeping a clean, well-maintained environment for your bunny and concentrating on solid nutrition will only make your rabbit healthier.

If you are well-prepared for the arrival of your bunny, both in terms of knowledge and equipment, you're about to embark on a grand adventure with an animal whose unique take on life -- by turns placid and, frankly, a little manic -- will delight you thoroughly from day one.

Relevant Websites

US Sites

House Rabbit Society
rabbit.org

My House Rabbit
www.myhouserabbit.com

The Bunny Guy – How to Successfully live indoors with a
pet rabbit
www.thebunnyguy.com

Pets at Home – Where Pets come first.
www.petsathome.com/webapp/wcs/stores/servlet/Info_106
01_rabbit-care-advice-home_-1_10551

MediRabbit - The Ultimate Rabbit Medicine Resource
www.medirabbit.com

American Rabbit Breeder's Association
www.arba.net

Association of Exotic Mammals Veterinarians
aemv.org

Relevant Websites

Rabbit Breeders England
rabbitbreeders.org.uk

The British Rabbit Council
www.thebrc.org

The Royal Society for the Prevention of Cruelty to
Animals/Rabbits
www.rspca.org.uk/allaboutanimals/pets

Frequently Asked Questions

How old should my rabbit be before I can have it spayed or neutered?

Females are sexually mature at 4 months of age, but most vets like to wait until they are at least 6 months old since surgery can be dangerous for younger animals.

Males can be neutered when their testicles descend at around 3.5 months of age.

Is it hard to litter train a rabbit?

Rabbits have natural habits and denning instincts that make litter training much easier. They do not like to do their "business" in the same place they eat and sleep.

They choose one or more places, often a corner, where they will urinate and leave pills routinely. If you put a litter box in that corner, the rabbit will use it.

Younger rabbits have a very short attention span, so stick with the training. If you adopt an older rabbit, you'll have no trouble getting your pet to use a litter box or boxes. Don't be surprised if you need multiple boxes.

Having your rabbit spayed or neutered at age 4-6 months is also helpful. They won't start marking their territory, and will be much more likely to use a litter box.

What are the major goals of rabbit proofing your house?

When you rabbit proof your home, you are not just attempting to protect your belongings, you are ensuring the safety of your companion bunny. At the same time that you need to provide your rabbit with a safe environment, you also need to give your pet suitable alternatives for the digging and chewing behaviors that are simply part of its nature as a rabbit.

Is any one part of rabbit proofing more important than any other?

At the top of your rabbit proofing list should be securing all electrical and telephone cords and making sure all toxic and potentially poisonous substances, including plants, are out of the rabbit's reach or out of its space entirely.

What do pet rabbits eat?

The fundamental elements of your pet's diet should include a high-quality brand of commercial rabbit pellets in combination with hay, fresh vegetables, and a constant supply of clean, fresh water.

What kind of vegetables should I give my rabbit and in what quantity?

Feed your rabbit one packed cup (136 g) of fresh vegetables per day per 2 pounds of the animal's body weight. See Appendix 4 for a list of suggested vegetables.

Frequently Asked Questions

Aren't cages or hutches with wire floors bad for rabbits?

Over time, a cage with a wire floor can seriously irritate a rabbit's feet, which do not have pads like those of a dog or cat. If you use a cage with a wire floor, you should provide your rabbit with a resting board or rug.

Slatted plastic floors or solid floors are fine, since a rabbit can very easily be trained to use a litter box.

How big should my rabbit's cage be?

The answer to cage size, with almost any kind of companion animal, is the bigger the better. Pick a cage that is 4-6 times larger than your rabbit when he is completely stretched out.

If your bunny has to be in its cage a large amount of the time, however, you will need to create more exercise space. Healthy rabbits need to run and play 2-5 hours a day in around 24 square feet of space (2.23m²).

Ideally, this is in a rabbit safe area in your home. If your rabbit is well trained, and your home is appropriately rabbit-proofed, this shouldn't be a problem.

Shouldn't my rabbit live outside?

In a word, no. The idea that rabbits are outside animals is badly outdated. A rabbit is a loving pet in need of as much or more companionship and interaction as a dog or cat.

Beyond the need for socialization and affection, rabbits can literally die of fright. The neighbor's dog or cat doesn't have to get inside your rabbit's hutch to kill it.

Other predators include possums, raccoons, skunks, and coyotes. Additionally, rabbits are very sensitive to heat, and can easily die on hot days.

Far from being a novelty notion, the idea of keeping a house rabbit is absolutely the best choice for these delightful, but sensitive creatures.

Why do rabbits chew all the time?

There are many reasons why rabbits chew. Understand that this is a normal activity, and one the rabbit enjoys. Your bunny isn't being "bad" when it chews, and shouldn't be punished. It's just being a rabbit!

For one thing, a rabbit's teeth continue to grow throughout their lives. They need appropriate things to chew on to keep their teeth trimmed down. If you can't handle the chewing, don't get a pet rabbit!

Why do rabbits dig?

Rabbits dig for the simple reason that they are burrowing animals by nature. They feel a natural instinct to dig into a burrow, which can get them into a lot of trouble if they mistake a recliner for a burrow!

Many bunny owners actually construct "tunnels" for their rabbits to simulate this very experience. Don't line the tunnel with carpet, however.

Rabbits will eat the indigestible carpet fibers, which can lead to life-threatening intestinal blockages. Again, don't "punish" your rabbit for digging. The animal is just doing what comes naturally.

What kind of toys do pet rabbits like?

Toys are an important part of your pet's life because they provide intellectual stimulation, physical exercise, and deflect your bunny's natural instinct to chew and dig toward acceptable channels.

Rabbits like cardboard boxes and paper bags. They love to shred anything, like an old copy of the phone book.

Most cat toys that roll or that can be tossed will attract their interest, as will hard plastic baby toys, ramps and constructs for climbing, and even something as simple as dried tree branches for gnawing.

(Avoid cherry, peach, apricot, plum, and redwood. All are toxic to rabbits.)

Should I get one rabbit or two?

In the wild, rabbits live in groups and have a deep-seated need for this kind of companionship. You can do a lot to satisfy your bunny's need for friendship, but bonded pairs are together constantly and communicate through an enormous vocabulary of body language as well as vocalizations.

Pairs of rabbits are, on a whole, easier to care for because they're happier and tend to get in less trouble out of depression and boredom. If you have the room, keeping a pair of rabbits is an excellent idea.

Rabbits are great with children, right?

Don't fall for the assumption that rabbits and children will automatically get along. Bunnies are not the placid, stationary creatures people think they are.

Young adult rabbits in particular are bundles of energy. Rabbits don't like sudden change, nor do they like to be approached loudly and quickly. They also don't like to be held. All of these things can lead to struggling, or defensive biting and kicking.

Rabbits can also suffer from stress-related illness to the point of death, and they are fragile creatures that must be handled correctly.

Rabbits will get along with the right children, but not all children are right for rabbits. You need to be extremely honest with yourself in evaluating your own children in this equation.

What about rabbits and other pets?

The same caveats apply to rabbits and other pets as to the discussion of rabbits and children above. Dogs and cats can literally scare rabbits to death if they are rough or simply omnipresent and constantly annoying or pestering the bunny.

That being said, larger rabbits can get enough and fight back. A mad rabbit can deliver a pretty wicked kick. Evaluate your existing pets with the same critical eye you should apply to your children and always put the needs of the rabbits first. They are the more sensitive creature in this consideration.

Rabbit Breeders Online by Breed - USA

American

www.roesbunnyfarm.weebly.com
www.broadriverpastures.com
www.freerangenh.com
www.spillmansrabbitry.com
www.stonewallrabbitry.com

American Chinchilla

www.humblebeginningsrabbitry.com
www.thesawyerfarms.com/rabbits/
www.suwaneecreekfarm.com
www.whitemorefarm.com
www.greatandsmallrabbitry.blogspot.com
www.greatandsmallrabbitry.blogspot.com
www.lapinofluxurysrabbitry.weebly.com

American Fuzzy Lop

www.urbanblissranch.weebly.com
www.fantasyhollandlopsrabbitry.weebly.com
www.bluewoodbunnies.com
www.fitzgeraldfamilyrabbitry.weebly.com
www.luvsomebunnyspecial.com
www.rubysrabbits.com
www.hollandlopsatnarrowgatefarm.com
www.hippityhoppartiesandmore.com
www.rebekahsrabbits.webs.com

www.strainshoneybunnies.com
www.ostararabbitry.com
www.freewebs.com/hollandlops

American Sable

www.mserabbitry.com
www.roesbunnyfarm.weebly.com
www.hotots-satins.com

Belgian Hare

www.amitypatchrabbits.com
www.hotots-satins.com

Beveren

www.suwaneecreekfarm.com
www.spillmansrabbitry.com

Blanc D'Hotot

www.dandbrabbit-tree.com
www.hotots-satins.com

Britannia Petite

www.tarmanfarm.com
www.krismosrabbitry.webs.com

Californian

www.azrabbits.com Monica Crocker
www.justfarmin.com
www.centralcoastrabbitry.weebly.com
www.sites.google.com/site/favettifamilyfarm/
www.shamrockrabbitry.weebly.com
www.roesbunnyfarm.weebly.com
www.high-plains.blogspot.com
www.oldsenfarm.com
www.hiddenoakrabbitry.webs.com
www.grizzlygiants.com
www.henrys-hares.yolasite.com
www.facebook.com/dragosbunnyfarm
www.pumpkinsrabbitry.webs.com
www.redbirdrabbitry.blogspot.com
www.lvrr.weebly.com
www.shamrockrabbits.com
www.macrabbitry.com
www.spillmansrabbitry.com
www.vicksrabbitry.com
www.songawayfarm.weebly.com
www.thorpcalifornians.wordpress.com
www.sliverpond.com
www.4ds-rabbitry.webs.com
www.oneacrefarmrabbits.com
www.2bucks&doe.com
www.montealmare.weebly.com
www.fuzzyvaughns.com
www.simplyllamas.com
www.desertkennels.com/desert-sage-rabbitry.html

Cavy

www.bluewoodbunnies.com
www.wellsrabbitry.webs.com
www.hazelhillcaviary.weebly.com
www.thorpcalifornians.wordpress.com
www.bettystlcdogtraining.com
www.snowmeadowfarm.weebly.com
www.littlepals.net

Champagne d'Argent

www.madhatterrabbits.wordpress.com
www.cuddlebunnysrabbitry.webs.com
www.roesbunnyfarm.weebly.com
www.jmsranchhome.com
www.harrisrabbitry.com
www.regalrabbits.com
www.lostspringrabbitry.com
www.freerangenh.com
www.redbirdrabbitry.blogspot.com
www.flatlandfarm.com
www.macrabbitry.com
www.vicksrabbitry.com
www.alltheragerabbitry.weebly.com
www.pixiehollowrabbitry.weebly.com

Checkered Giant

www.daybreakrabbitry.webs.com

Cinnamon

www.madhatterrabbits.wordpress.com
www.oaktreerabbitry.com
www.daybreakrabbitry.webs.com
www.mollogontailsrabbitry.com

Commerical

www.roesbunnyfarm.weebly.com
www.lvrr.weebly.com
www.oneacrefarmrabbits.com
www.desertkennels.com/desert-sage-rabbitry.html

Crème d'Argent

www.cuddlebunnysrabbitry.webs.com
www.roesbunnyfarm.weebly.com
www.thedancingfarmer.com
www.flatlandfarm.com
www.freerangenh.com
www.montealmare.weebly.com

Dutch

www.centralcoastrabbitry.weebly.com
www.oldsenfarm.com
www.rockatsouthwind.com
www.trevorsstarbucksanddoes.weebly.com
www.happyvalleyrabbitry.com
www.thorpcalifornians.wordpress.com

www.freewebs.com/painted_whiskers_rabbitry
www.freewebs.com/painted_whiskers_rabbitry
www.rebekahsrabbits.webs.com
www.plumhillfarm.webs.com

Dwarf Hotot

www.bunnycentral.com
www.rockin'horseacres.com
www.hippityhoppartiesandmore.com
www.rebekahsrabbits.webs.com
www.alltheragerabbitry.weebly.com
www.pixiehollowrabbitry.weebly.com
www.kbrabbit.com

English Angora

www.thefairhare.com
www.justfarmin.com
www.angoracouture.com
www.24karrotrabbits.com
www.bunnycentral.com
www.alpacaobsession.com
www.melynn.webs.com
www.sites.google.com/site/lanajouraangora/
www.greenesgardenthings.com
www.evergreenfarm.biz
www.heartfelthares.com
www.ourlibertyhillfarm.com
www.hippityhoppartiesandmore.com
www.beaconbendalpacas.com

www.hiddenvalleyrabbitry.weebly.com
www.bunnytrailbunnies.weebly.com

English Lop

www.hoppylops.com
www.lopsofluv.weebly.com
www.appleshirerabbits.com
www.mybunniesgalore.com
www.fourbrabbitry.webs.com
www.jennaslittlerabbitry.webs.com
www.lonepinerabbitry.com

English Spot

www.urbanblissranch.weebly.com
www.melynn.webs.com
www.sinkhollowfarm.com
www.henrys-hares.yolasite.com
www.facebook.com/dragosbunnyfarm
www.freewebs.com/bbfarms

Flemish Giant

www.justfarmin.com
www.thewildwoodsrabbitry.com
www.weedflemishgiantrabbitry.com
www.preciousjewellsrabbitry.com
www.buckandheelranch.com
www.jmsranchhome.com
www.lbrabbitry.webs.com

www.oldsenfarm.com
www.lbrabbitry.webs.com
www.melynn.webs.com
www.hoppylops.com
www.regalrabbits.com
www.gentlegiantrabbitry.com
www.grizzlygiants.com
www.sinkhollowfarm.com
ww.greenesgardenthings.com
www.facebook.com/dragosbunnyfarm
www.cajuncottontails.host-ed.me
www.halfpinthaven.com
www.staylorsbbfarm.webs.com
www.sites.google.com/site/vortexhollowflemishfarm/
www.snuggliesburrow.com
www.stonewallrabbitry.com
www.redriverrabbitry.com
www.ostararabbitry.com

Florida White

www.roesbunnyfarm.weebly.com
www.tarmanfarm.com

French Angora

www.pennydownfarm.com
www.fmicrofarm.com
www.cloudyshoreangoras.wordpress.com
www.rocksoupranch.com
www.melynn.webs.com

www.dbaretfarm.weebly.com
www.heartsongrabbitry.com

French Lop

www.lynnsrabbits.com
www.fitzgeraldfamilyrabbitry.weebly.com
www.hippityhoppartiesandmore.com
www.fourbrabbitry.webs.com
www.kbrabbit.com

Giant Angora

www.melynn.webs.com
www.bluewoodbunnies.com
www.evergreenfarm.biz
www.ourlibertyhillfarm.com
www.fuzzyvaughns.com

Giant Chinchilla

www.justfarmin.com
www.alpacaobsession.com
www.lapinofluxurysrabbitry.weebly.com

Harlequin

www.melynn.webs.com
www.bluewoodbunnies.com

Havana

www.daybreakrabbitry.webs.com
www.thorpcalifornians.wordpress.com

Himalayan

www.high-plains.blogspot.com
www.oldsenfarm.com
www.henrys-hares.yolasite.com
www.bluewoodbunnies.com
www.shinysatins.weebly.com
www.hoppinhimalayans.com

Holland Lop

www.sgthoppersrabbitry.com
www.softpawsrabbits.weebly.com
www.thebunnygardenrabbitry.com
www.madhatterrabbits.wordpress.com
www.zinnsrabbitfarm.com
www.tophopsrabbitry.weebly.com
www.cmhopnround.com/home.html
www.hollandloptophatrabbitry.com
www.fantasyhollandlopsrabbitry.weebly.com
www.loveablelopsnlions.weebly.com
www.huntershollandlops.com
www.woodlandrabbitry.com
www.pjspetsitting.com/JasonsHollands.htm
www.chasehillrabbitry.com
www.lollilopsrabbitry.weebly.com

www.classicimagerabbitry.com
www.lynnsrabbits.com
www.ritchelsrabbitry.webs.com
www.smokywoodsrabbitry.weebly.com
www.maryshoneybunnies.com
www.susieslittlestlops.weebly.com
www.leaningtreeacres.blogspot.com
www.trevorsstarbucksanddoes.weebly.com
www.pridenjoyrabbitry.webs.com
www.freewebs.com/bbfarms
www.ainsleywillowrabbits.weebly.com
www.bundlesofbunniesrabbitry.weebly.com
www.fitzgeraldfamilyrabbitry.weebly.com
www.fluffybunnyrabbitry.com
www.wellsrabbitry.webs.com
www.greatandsmallrabbitry.blogspot.com
www.gumtreehollowrabbitry.webs.com
www.wtfrabbits.com
www.shamrockrabbits.com
www.luvlops.com
www.bunnyblueeyes.com
www.fortheloveofsandyrabbitry.com
www.mollogontailsrabbitry.com
www.thelookingglassrabbitry.com
www.mybunniesgalore.com
www.luvsomebunnyspecial.com
www.mysticwarrenrabbitry.com
www.heartfelthares.com
www.rubysrabbits.com
www.happyvalleyrabbitry.com
www.hollandlopsatnarrowgatefarm.com

www.hippityhoppartiesandmore.com
www.sugarhillhollands.webs.com
www.stonehillrabbitry.com
www.hoppinglops.webs.com
www.rebekahsrabbits.webs.com
www.alltheragerabbitry.weebly.com
www.bunnytrailbunnies.weebly.com
www.pixiehollowrabbitry.weebly.com
www.cloverridgehollands.com
www.avatarhollands.com
www.hippityhoprabbits.com
www.sites.google.com/site/scarletknighthollands/
www.m-mheritagefarm.com
www.strainshoneybunnies.com
www.midnightmoonrabbitry.com
www.wix.com/quietcreek/quietcreek-farm
www.pwfarmtexas.com
www.dandbrabbit-tree.com
www.countryrabbitfarm.com
www.kbrabbit.com
www.honeyvillehollands.webs.com
www.gioshollandlops.com
www.larueswascawwywabbits.com
www.beautifulrunrabbitry.weebly.com
www.hopnhollands.com
www.dragonflyhollands.com
www.lionheartrabbitry.com
www.freewebs.com/hollandlops

Jersey Wooly

www.24karrotrabbits.com
www.fancyrabbits.com
www.freewebs.com/bunnyhollow
www.melynn.webs.com
www.safehavenrabbitry.com
www.bluewoodbunnies.com
www.freewebs.com/bbfarms
www.wellsrabbitry.webs.com
www.heartfelthares.com
www.hiddenvalleyrabbitry.weebly.com
www.kbrabbit.com
www.wix.com/quietcreek/quietcreek
www.dandbrabbit-tree.com
www.lionheartrabbitry.com

Lilac

lupinlapinrabbitry.weebly.com

Mini Lop

www.sgthoppersrabbitry.com
www.bunnycentral.com
www.heartsongrabbitry.com
www.daybreakrabbitry.webs.com
www.bundlesofbunniesrabbitry.weebly.com
www.fitzgeraldfamilyrabbitry.weebly.com
www.heminirabbitry.vpweb.com
www.fourbrabbitry.webs.com

www.hippityhoppartiesandmore.com
www.winterbrookrabbits.com
www.rebekahsrabbits.webs.com
www.pennyhillrabbitry.weebly.com
www.kbrabbit.com
www.lonepinerabbitry.com

Mini Rex

www.softpawsrabbits.weebly.com
www.madhatterrabbits.wordpress.com
www.sites.google.com/site/favettifamilyfarm/
www.cuddlebunnysrabbitry.webs.com
www.roesbunnyfarm.weebly.com
www.bunnycentral.com
www.high-plains.blogspot.com
www.thesawyerfarms.com/rabbits/
www.lynnsrabbits.com
www.heirloomhares.webs.com
www.hiddenoakrabbitry.webs.com
www.amitypatchrabbits.com
www.facebook.com/dragosbunnyfarm
www.freewebs.com/bbfarms
www.rabbittree.us
www.wellsrabbitry.webs.com
www.allegianceminirex.com
www.halfpinthaven.com
www.leapyearrabbitry.weebly.com
www.heminirabbitry.vpweb.com
www.mysticwarrenrabbitry.com
www.happyvalleyrabbitry.com

www.hippityhoppartiesandmore.com
www.mollogontailsrabbitry.com
www.fourbrabbitry.webs.com
www.eliteminirex.com
www.tarmanfarm.com
www.windwalkerrabbitry.com
www.freewebs.com/painted_whiskers_rabbitry
www.pennyhillrabbitry.weebly.com
www.dandbrabbit-tree.com
www.kbrabbit.com
www.beautifulrunrabbitry.weebly.com
www.cgrabbitry.webs.com
www.freewebs.com/hollandlops

Mini Satin

www.fieldstonerabbitry.weebly.com
www.oaktreerabbitry.com
www.sdrabbitry.com
www.2bucks&doe.com
www.hotots-satins.com

Netherland Satin

www.mamachoorabbitry.webs.com
www.fancyrabbits.com
www.centralcoastrabbitry.weebly.com
www.sites.google.com/site/favettifamilyfarm/
www.tophopsrabbitry.weebly.com
www.preciousjewellsrabbitry.com
www.shamrockrabbitry.weebly.com

www.cuddlebunnysrabbitry.webs.com
www.bunnycentral.com
www.loveablelopsnlions.weebly.com
www.spumantirabbitry.com
www.lynnsrabbits.com
www.hiddenoakrabbitry.webs.com
www.facebook.com/wascallywabbitsofga
www.smokywoodsrabbitry.weebly.com
www.susieslittlestlops.weebly.com
www.leaningtreeacres.blogspot.com
www.greenesgardenthings.com
www.pridenjoyrabbitry.webs.com
www.sdrabbitry.com
www.fluffybunnyrabbitry.com
www.wellsrabbitry.webs.com
www.rockin'horseacres.com
www.wtfrabbits.com
www.bunnyblueeyes.com
www.syracuse-rabbit.com
www.hippityhoppartiesandmore.com
www.zwergeland.com
www.redgaterabbitranch.com
www.lglazier@embarqmail.com
www.hiddenvalleyrabbitry.weebly.com
www.shadythicket.weebly.com
www.pixiehollowrabbitry.weebly.com
www.countryrabbitfarm.com
www.kbrabbit.com
www.dandbrabbit-tree.com
www.larueswascawwywabbits.com
www.beautifulrunrabbitry.weebly.com

New Zealand

www.sgthoppersrabbitry.com
www.justfarmin.com
www.roesbunnyfarm.weebly.com
www.facebook.com/fogcityrabbitry
www.chasehillrabbitry.com
www.thesawyerfarms.com/rabbits/
www.harrisrabbitry.com
www.littlethumperrabbitry.weebly.com
www.lynnsrabbits.com
www.grizzlygiants.com
www.oldhighway30rabbitry.com
www.susieslittlestlops.weebly.com
www.facebook.com/dragosbunnyfarm
www.freerangenh.com
www.rabbittree.us
www.redbirdrabbitry.blogspot.com
www.lvrr.weebly.com
wwww.songawayfarm.weebly.com
www.macrabbitry.com
www.spillmansrabbitry.com
www.vicksrabbitry.com
www.strainshoneybunnies.com
www.oneacrefarmrabbits.com
www.montealmare.weebly.com
www.hippityhoprabbitry@gmail.com
www.desertkennels.com/desert-sage-rabbitry.html

Palomino

www.oldsenfarm.com
www.mollogontailsrabbitry.com

Polish

www.bunnybarnfarms.com
www.sdrabbitry.com
www.oaktreerabbitry.com
www.bundlesofbunniesrabbitry.weebly.com
www.wtfrabbits.com
www.lvrr.weebly.com
www.freewebs.com/painted_whiskers_rabbitry
www.esthersrabbits.com
www.wix.com/quietcreek/quietcreek
www.dandbrabbit-tree.com

Rex

www.softpawsrabbits.weebly.com
www.madhatterrabbits.wordpress.com
www.rexrabbits4you.com
www.oldsenfarm.com
www.melynn.webs.com
www.freerangenh.com
www.vicksrabbitry.com
www.ayrerabbitry.webs.com
www.4ds-rabbitry.webs.com
www.oneacrefarmrabbits.com
www.desertkennels.com/desert-sage-rabbitry.html

Rheinlander

www.madhatterrabbits.wordpress.com
www.hollandlopsatnarrowgatefarm.com

Satin

www.madhatterrabbits.wordpress.com
www.rocksoupranch.com
www.oldsenfarm.com
www.dbaretfarm.weebly.com
www.oaktreerabbitry.com
www.metzgerbunnyfarm.com
www.snowwhitesdwarfsrabbitry.com
www.snowwhitesdwarfsrabbitry.com
www.songawayfarm.weebly.com
www.mollogontailsrabbitry.com
www.4ds-rabbitry.webs.com
www.thegreenvalleystables.com
www.jensrabbits@live.com
www.shinysatins.weebly.com
www.hotots-satins.com
www.desertkennels.com/desert-sage-rabbitry.html

Satin Angora

www.melynn.webs.com
www.dbaretfarm.weebly.com
www.heartsongrabbitry.com
www.evergreenfarm.biz
www.beaconbendalpacas.com

www.fuzzyvaughns.com

Silver Fox

www.madhatterrabbits.wordpress.com
www.classicimagerabbitry.com
www.thedancingfarmer.com
www.broadriverpastures.com
www.freerangenh.com
www.whitemorefarm.com
www.lvrr.weebly.com
www.redbirdrabbitry.blogspot.com
www.spillmansrabbitry.com
www.pinesrabbitry.webs.com
www.ayrerabbitry.webs.com
www.4ds-rabbitry.webs.com
www.thegreenvalleystables.com
www.oserssilverfoxrabbitry.com
www.seasiderabbits.weebly.com
www.montealmare.weebly.com

Silver Marten

www.madhatterrabbits.wordpress.com
www.metzgerbunnyfarm.com
www.redbirdrabbitry.blogspot.com
www.mollogontailsrabbitry.com
Standard Chinchilla

www.tarmanfarm.com
www.lapinofluxurysrabbitry.weebly.com

Tan

www.oldsenfarm.com
www.blueribbonrabbitry.com
www.urbanrabbits.net
www.hiddenvalleyrabbitry.weebly.com
www.alltheragerabbitry.weebly.com
www.larueswascawwywabbits.com
www.lonepinerabbitry.com

Thrianta

www.hoppylops.com

Rabbit Breeders Online – UK

www.myker.co.uk

www.rabbitmanor.weebly.com

www.freewebs.com/christiesfrenchlops

www.bellabunnylops.co.uk

www.littlelandbunnys.co.uk

www.jessica-rabbits.weebly.com

lealuulops.webs.com

www.freewebs.co.uk/hannahsbunnies

www.craigelachiestud.webs.com

www.paganrose.co.uk

sparklesatin.moonfruit.com

www.mini-lops.webs.com

poppyshappybunnies.webs.com

www.curlywhiskers-rabbitry

www.jensbunnies.weebly.com

www.yorkshire-minilops.co.uk

www.freewebs.com/lowreylops

www.nikniastud.co.uk

www.therabbitsden.co.uk

hiphopsbunnies.weebly.com

www.eliterabbitstud.co.uk

sycamorebunnies.webs.com

www.pasturelops.webs.com

www.sunflowernurseryrabbits.co.uk

ryanrabbitstud.webs.com

www.longlandfrenchlops.webs.com

www.cottontail-lodge.co.uk

www.happy-hoppers.co.uk

www.northwestpets.co.uk

www.englishrabbit.org.uk

www.redbeck-orchard.info

lealuulops.webs.com

www.freewebs.com/rexmadness

llan-minilops.webs.com

heathersminilops.weebly.com

www.thehappyrabbitfamily.webs.com

daisymeadowwarren.moonfruit.com

www.freewebs.com/cathyshires

www.spencersbunnies.piczo.com

www.eloquencestud.moonfruit.com

www.brownsbunnies.webs.com

bluemoonbunnies.webs.com

Rabbit Breeders Online – Canada

aliyahsangelscaviary.webs.com

www.compactcrittersrabbitry.com

www.devonglen.com

fenwoodhobbyfarm.webs.com

fuzziewasie.webs.com

jacknwysrabbits.weebly.com

legacyrabbitry.ca

pine-river.tripod.com

rjrabbitry.webs.com

raysskinnyguinea.weebly.com

www.redvelvetrabbitry.weebly.com

rigidstonerabbitry.webs.com

shadowcreekrabbitry.weebly.com

www.freewebs.com/shannondoerabbitry

sunnyheights.tripod.com

www.sunnymeadowscages.com

www.windingpathcreations.com

www.trinitytrailteddies.com

www.tursaco.com

Appendix 1– ARBA Show Standard

Source: www.arba.net/PDFs/Showmanship.pdf

American Rabbit Breeders Assn.
PO Box 5667, Bloomington, IL 61702
309-664-7500 info@ARBA.net

Rabbit Showmanship

General Note to Judge: Judge the contestants actions and knowledge. Do not judge the behavior or condition of the rabbit.

Carry - Proper support, maintain control. Points: 5

Pose - Correct pose for breed. Introduction - greeting/name, step back. Points: 5

Pose Terms - Breed, compact, cylindrical, full arch, mandolin, semi-arch, commercial. Points: 2

Ears - Check both ears. Read tattoo. Points: 3

Ear Terms - Mites, canker, carriage, thickness, color torn or missing portions, fur covering. Points: 2

Turn Over - Smooth motion, proper control, rest weight on table. Points: 5

Eyes - Properly open eyes, not forcing open. Points: 3

Eye Terms - Proper color, blindness, wall eye, moon eye, weepy eye or signs of conjunctivitis. Points: 2

Nose - Proper hand position. Show both nostrils. Check inside legs for nasal discharge. Points: 3

Nose Terms - Snuffles, nasal discharge, foreign spots or colors. Points: 2

Teeth - Proper hand position. Show upper and lower incisors. Points: 3

Teeth Terms - Malocclusion, buck teeth, wolf teeth, peg teeth, broken teeth. Points: 2

Front Feet / Legs - Check straightness of legs. Check toenails, pad, and dewclaw. Proper thumb position. Points: 3

Front Feet / Leg Terms - Broken, extra and missing toes, mismatched, white, missing toenails, bone density, dewclaw, pads. Points: 2

Belly - Check under jaw and chest. Check abdomen and sides. Smooth and complete coverage. Points: 3

Belly Terms - Abscess, tumor, abnormalities, pigeon breast, blemishes, mastitis. Points: 2

Rear Feet / Legs - Check straightness of legs. Check toenails and hocks. Proper thumb position. Points: 3

Rear Feet / Legs Terms - Broken and missing toes, mismatched, white, missing toenails, bone density, straightness, sore hocks. Points: 2

Sex - Proper position of rabbit and hand. Expose vent / penis and testicles. Points: 3

Sex Terms - Buck/Doe, vent disease, hutch burn, split penis, descended testicles in Int/Sr. Points: 2

Tail - Extend tail. Move side to side. Examine underside. Points: 3

Tail Terms - Wry, dead, bobbed, broken, color, straightness. Points: 2

Fur - Return to pose. Smooth motion. Proper control. Stroke coat from tail to head to show fur type. Points: 3

Fur Terms - Density, texture, sheen, luster, rollback, flyback, rex, standing, wool, undercolor, ring color, surface color, molt. Points: 2

Judging Comments - Final pose. Head, ears, shoulder, chest, midsection, loin, hindquarters, rump, breed specific. (markings/color) Points: 10

Judging Comment Terms - Excellent, good, fair, poor, balance, condition, finish. Do not use word "nice!" Points: 5

Overall Presentation - Show coat / apron / long sleeves. Smile. Hair neat. No rings. No dangling jewelry. No gum. Points: 5

Overall Presentation Terms - Humane treatment. Controls animal at all times. Good eye contact. Follows directions. Thanks judge. Points: 5

Knowledge - Answers to questions. Points: 10

Total Possible Points: 100

Appendix 2– BRC Breed Standards

Source: thebrc.org/standards.htm

The current edition of the Standard book for The British Rabbit Council covers the period 2011-2016. A copy of the book, complete with photos, may be purchased at the Council's website.

Because the breed standards are extensive, they will not be reproduced here. Please visit thebrc.org to view or download the applicable PDFs. The currently listed breeds are.

Section F - Fancy Breeds

Angora
Dutch
Dutch Tri-coloured (R.V.)
English
Flemish Giant
Giant Papillon (R.V.)
Hare Belgian
Hare Tan
Harlequin
Himalayan
Lionhead
Netherland Dwarf
Polish
Rhinelander (R.V.)
Silver

Tan
Thrianta (R.V.)
Tri-coloured English (R.V.)
Black Hare

Section L - Lop Breeds

Lop Cashmere
Lop Cashmere Miniature
Lop Dwarf
Lop English
Lop French
Lop German
Lop Meissner (R.V.)
Lop Miniature
Lop Miniature Lion

Section N - Normal Fur Breeds

Alaska
Argente Bleu
Argente Brun
Argente Creme
Argente de Champagne
Argente Noir
Beige (R.V.)
Beveren
Blac de Bouscat (R.V.)
Blanc de Hotot (R.V.)
Blanc de Termonde (R.V.)
British Giant

Californian
Chinchilla
Chinchilla Giganta
Continental Giant coloured
Continental Giant white
Deilenaar (R.V.)
Fox - Silver
Golden Glavcot (R.V.)
Havana
Hulstlander (R.V.)
Lilac
NZ White, black, blue
NZ Red
Perifee (R.V.)
Pointed Beveren (R.V.)
Siamese Sable - Marten Sable
Sallander (R.V.)
Satin
Siberian
Smoke Pearl
Squirrel (R.V.)
Sussex (R.V.)
Swiss Fox (R.V.)
Thuringer (R.V.)
Vienna Coloured (R.V.)
Vienna White (R.V.)
Wheaten (R.V.)
Wheaten Lynx (R.V.)
Fauve de Bourgogne (R.V.)
Argente St. Hubert
Miniature Satin

Section R - Rex

General Standard
Self - Black, Blue, Ermine, Havana, Lilac, Nutria
Shaded - Sable Siamese, Seal Siamese, Smoke Pearl, Smoke
Pearl Marten, Tortoiseshell
Tan Pattern - Fawn, Fox, Sable Marten, Seal Marten,
Orange, Otter, Tan
Agouti Pattern - Castor, Chinchilla, Cinnamon, Lynx, Opal
Other Varieties - Dalmatian, Harlequin, Himalayan, Silver
Seal, Satin Rex
Rough Coated - Astrex
Rough Coated - Opossum
Mini Rex
Mini Rex Broken

Appendix 3 - Suggested Vegetables for Your Rabbit

Source: Susan A. Brown, DVM, "Suggested Vegetables and Fruits for a Rabbit Diet," House Rabbit Society, 12 April 2012, rabbit.org/suggested-vegetables-and-fruits-for-a-rabbit-diet/

Fresh vegetables should make up about 75% of your pet rabbit's diet. A good formula to follow is 1 packed cup (136 g) of vegetables per 2 pounds (0.9 kg) of the animal's body weight per day.

Remember, rabbits are crepuscular. They feed at dawn and dusk and do not need to graze all day.

The following leafy greens are high in oxalic acid, which, if feed excessively over time, can cause kidney damage. These foods are very nutritious, and if dispensed appropriately, are a healthy part of a rabbit's diet. For every four types of greens given a rabbit per day, only one should be taken from this list.

Beet Greens
Mustard Greens
Parsley
Radish Tops
Spinach
Swiss Chard

Appendix 3 - Suggested Vegetables for Your Rabbit

These leafy greens are low in oxalic acid.

Arugula
Basil
Bok Choy
Borage leaves
Carrot tops
Chicory
Cilantro
Cucumber leaves
Dandelion greens
Dill leaves
Endive
Ecarole
Fennel (leaves and base)
Frisee Lettuce
Kale
Mache
Mint
Radicchio
Raspberry leaves
Red or green lettuce
Romaine lettuce
Spring greens
Turnip greens
Watercress
Wheatgrass

About 15% of your pet's diet should be drawn from non-leafy vegetables. This equals roughly 1 tablespoon (15 g) per 2 pounds (0.9 kg) of body weight daily.)

Bell Peppers
Broccoli
Brussel sprouts
Cabbage
Carrots
Celery
Summer Squash
Zucchini

Give your rabbit only 10% fruit, or roughly 1 teaspoon (5 g) per 2 pounds (0.9 kg) of body weight per day. Wash all fruit thoroughly.

If you have any concerns about chemicals, remove the skin, although in general, it is more nutritious to leave the skin intact.

Apples
Apricot
Berries
Kiwi
Mango
Nectarine
Papaya
Peeled Banana
Pear
Peach
Pitted Plums
Pitted Cherries

Appendix 3 - Suggested Vegetables for Your Rabbit

Glossary

A

abscess - A swelling containing dense pus in the mouth or on the body of a rabbit (or any small animal) surrounded by inflamed skin. Will often by hard and feel hot. Surgical removal may be necessary to treat the lesion.

adult - For the purposes of showing a rabbit, the animal must be 6 months or older for some classes, and 8 months for others to be considered an adult.

albino - Rabbits with white fur and pink or red eyes.

amoxicillin - A common prescribed antibiotic for small animal species that can be fatal if used with rabbits.

anal glands - A pair of scent glands located on either side of the genitals subject to the build-up of a pungent, oily, brown substance that should be cleaned away regularly.

ARBA - Acronym for the American Rabbit Breeders Association, the governing body of rabbit fanciers in the United States, which publishes a book of breed standards.

B

bangs - In some breeds this is the long wool that appears at the top of the head and at the base of the ears in the front.

banding - Any shaft of hair marked with various colors in bands from the base to the tip.

base color - The shade of color of the fur lying closest to a rabbit's skin.

back - The upper portion of a rabbit's body running from the neck down to the tail.

belly - The lower part of a rabbit's body running from the forelegs across the abdomen to the crotch.

belly color - The coloration of fur on a rabbit's underside from the forelegs to the crotch.

binky - An exuberant leap with mid-air twists denoting happiness and playfulness.

breed - Any group of domestic rabbits that can reproduce for distinct characteristics in regard to body shape and size, marking, fur, and temperament.

breeder - Any person that specializes in raising a particular variety or varieties of rabbit.

C

cecal pellets - Partially digested food secreted by the rabbit for re-ingestion to achieve maximum nutritional value. Also called cecatropes and night droppings.

Glossary

chest - The front portion of a rabbit's body limited to the area between the forelegs and under the neck.

chinning- When a rabbit rubs its face against a piece of furniture or any other object to place its mark of ownership.

cobby - A body configuration that is stocky and somewhat stout with short legs.

crown - Located at the top of the head and between the base of the ear in some lop-eared breeds, this is a basal ridge of cartilage.

D

dew claw - The extra toe on the inside of the front leg of a rabbit that serves no function.

doe - An intact female rabbit that has not been spayed.

F

flank - The sides of the rabbit located above the belly and between the hips and ribs.

flattening - A flattening of the body and lowering of the ears in an attempt to hide. Signals fear.

foot - That portion of the leg on which the rabbit stands. On the front legs it's below the ankle, on the rear leg below the hock joint.

forehead - The portion of the head located in the front and lying between the eyes and the base of the ears.

forequarters - The section of the body that begins at the next and extends backward to the last rib.

G

gestation - The length of time a doe carries young rabbits in her uterus. Typically 28-32 days.

H

hare - Hares are kin to rabbits, in that they are both members of the order Lagomorpha. Hares, however, are not domesticated. They are larger, faster, have big bag feet, and stronger hind legs.

hindquarters - The back or posterior region of the body comprised of the loins, hips, hind legs, and rump.

hip - The first joint of the hind leg and the thigh joint.

hock - On the hind leg, the middle section or joint located between the hip and foot.

I

inner ear - The inner portion of the ear that is curved or concave.

intact - A rabbit that retains its functioning reproductive organs.

K

kit - The term for a baby rabbit.

knee - The second leg joint that connects the leg and thigh. In animals, it is called the hock on the hind legs, and the elbow on the front legs.

L

litter - A group of baby rabbits born to one mother at one time.

loin - The loins are located on either side of the spine between the lower rib and hip joint.

M

malocclusion - A inherited condition in which the upper and lower jaws are malformed so that the teeth do not meet. Results in uneven teeth that grow too long and extend out of the mouth.

molt - The periodic shedding of the rabbit's fur. Occurs at least twice a year, or every 3-4 months with some rabbits.

muzzle - The portion of the head including the nose, mouth, and lower jaw that project forward from the face.

N

neck - The portion of the rabbit that connects the body and head.

nest box - A box placed inside the enclosure for the purpose of sleeping or as a place for a pregnant doe to give birth.

neutering - The surgical removal of a male's reproductive organs.

P

paunch - The portion of the abdomen on rabbits that tends to be prominent.

pyrethrum - A chemical agent in many commercial flea control products that has been found to cause adverse neurological reactions in many small animals.

R

rabbitry - Any place where domestic rabbits are kept for pleasure or business purposes.

ribs - The portion of the body on the side behind the shoulder and above the body where the ribcage is located. Curved in appearance.

S

saddle - The intermediate portion of the back between the shoulder and loin that is rounded.

shoulder - The last and uppermost joint of the front leg, connecting the limb with the body.

snuffle - The rabbit equivalent of kennel cough. An upper respiratory condition similar to the common cold.

spaying - The surgical removal of a female's reproductive organs.

spraying - The expulsion of pungent urine by intact males as a territorial marker.

squatting - When a rabbit is sitting on all four feet with ears at "half mast." A calm position with no fear present.

U

under color - The color of the fur shaft lying closest to the skin. This is not a reference to the color of the rabbit's belly.

uterus - The organ in female mammals where babies are carried until they are ready to be born.

W

walking dandruff - The common term for fur mites. See Chapter 4 - Rabbit Health for more information.

weaning - The process by which young rabbits begin to take solid food rather than their mother's milk. Generally occurs around 4 and 8 weeks.

Index

Index

Index